Personal Finance for Young Professionals

Personal Finance for Young Professionals

Scott Gong

BEP
BUSINESS EXPERT PRESS
Leader in applied, concise business books

First published in 2025 by
Business Expert Press, LLC
222 East 46th Street, New York, NY 10017
www.businessexpertpress.com

ISBN-13: 978-1-63742-898-6 (paperback)
ISBN-13: 978-1-63742-899-3 (e-book)

Finance and Financial Management Collection

First edition: 2025

10 9 8 7 6 5 4 3 2 1

EU SAFETY REPRESENTATIVE
Mare Nostrum Group B.V.
Mauritskade 21D
1091 GC Amsterdam
The Netherlands
gpsr@mare-nostrum.co.uk

Contents

List of Figures and Tables

Figures

Tables

Description

Personal Finance for Young Professionals presents a combination of refreshing psychological perspectives alongside practical analytical examples. Readers will learn to understand their money philosophy while developing an intentional financial system that works for their current lifestyle, risk tolerance, and long-term financial goals.

In lieu of the plethora of detail presented in this book, I can summarize "how to be successful with your finances" on a single sheet of paper. There isn't much to it, but it takes more than a generic plan. The system must be able to be adjusted to meet the needs of unique individuals. This book provides the appropriate level of detail to help young professionals make the right financial decisions for themselves while cultivating the necessary mindset to stick with their plan in the long run. Notable topics include budgeting, financial organization, credit, debt, taxes, investing, retirement, and homebuying.

Over the past several years, the contents of this book have been discussed with industry folks, friends, family, students, and acquaintances. These discussions provided the author with a holistic understanding of people's relationships with money and helped him develop a teachable approach to personal finance. The author draws on over a decade of tutoring experience to break down the complexity of personal finance into easily digestible and applicable kernels of knowledge.

Dedication

Dedicated to everyone who let me peer into their financial situation—your insights have provided me with the perspective and motivation to write this book for young professionals.

Review Quotes

"*Be not afraid: Even if you have a seemingly genetic aversion or allergy to financial planning in all forms, this book is for you. With* Personal Finance for Young Professionals, *Scott Gong offers a light in the darkness, destigmatizing the daunting processes of money management with humor, intelligence, and the reassurance and encouragement the most skeptical and intimidated among us need. And if you're already interested and amenable, all the better: This book will take you from novice to pro, dabbler to badass, faster and more accurately than ChatGPT.*"—**Brit Washburn, editor and author of *Notwithstanding, Homing In,* and *What Is Given***

"'*The dog ate my homework has never been a wealth-building strategy. As a young professional, the time is now to develop the discipline to respect your money and build a life on your terms. In an era filled with information overload and the siren songs of doom spending,* Personal Finance for Young Professionals *cuts through all the noise with key principles, actionable examples, and practical exercises. Scott's guidance even helped to give me the tools to launch my own business. It's your call to learn now or forever play catchup.*"—**London England, Scott's former student and colleague**

"*I really appreciated the conversational tone and relatable stories throughout the book—it felt like sitting down with a friend who's openly sharing their journey. Scott comes across as deeply human, and his story is a powerful reminder that financial empowerment is within reach for young professionals from all backgrounds.*"—**Verica Nakeva, licensed realtor**

"*Personal finance is one of the most important life skills that is never taught in schools, and many personal finance books are filled with bad ideas and get-rich-quick schemes. Scott's thoughtful little book is completely different. From the stock market to retiring, it gives its readers the tools to be confident in their financial future, regardless of political outcomes.*"—**Zach Kluver, Editor at *Quantum Commodity Intelligence***

Preface

Welcome to *Personal Finance for Young Professionals!* Have you ever stressed about money or been unsure about a financial decision? Whether you make a lot of money or a little, financial stress affects everyone—some from a very young age.

In this book, we will cover key financial topics that are relevant to young professionals, such as investing, budgeting, credit, taxes, homebuying, and more. The goal of this text is to introduce you to all of the tools, caveats, rules of thumb, analyses, and reasoning necessary to make informed decisions about your finances. This book will *not* tell you exactly what you need to do to be financially successful; instead, we will walk through what it takes to develop a financial foundation and strategy and then understand how various choices will impact your finances and your life. Financial success and security look different to everybody and can be achieved in a multitude of ways. Rather than following an inflexible plan, it is best to understand the tools at your disposal that can be used to create a plan that fits your desired lifestyle and long-term goals.

The truth is that the vast majority of adults are undereducated about finances. How many adults have you known who looked like they had it all figured out but ended up having to work until they were too old to move? How many people do you know who don't even know approximately how much they spend in a year? How many people have you met who have to wait until pay day to buy groceries? How many people do you know who have financial regrets? How many people do you know who cannot cover a $500 emergency without going into debt?

It is not entirely their fault—personal finance is unfortunately not commonly taught in school or in our lives. Most people grow up relying on learning from others, who learned from others before them. The result of this eternal game of telephone is information that might not be 100% factual. Even if the information is factual, it may not apply to your specific situation or there may be caveats that were lost in translation. When you learn through the grapevine, you don't learn the mathematical reasoning behind what you're learning, and that is a recipe for disaster because you may never be able to make a truly knowledgeable decision independently.

There is *always* a mathematically optimal way to manage your finances, and understanding the reasoning behind why a particular approach is optimal will allow you to make the most informed decisions. Understanding the math will allow you to determine where that tipping point is and how to calculate precisely how much you will sacrifice when selecting a suboptimal option, which is not the end of the world! Life is all about making decisions with your limited personal resources to bring about the greatest measure of happiness *for you*. Turns out life and economics are one and the same, except that you don't live your life in a spreadsheet. A financially suboptimal choice may in fact bring you more happiness and, therefore, greater quality of life, which can often outweigh a small financial inefficiency. At the end of the day, understanding the mathematical, psychological, and subsequent financial implications of a decision can help you take your personal finance game—and life—to the next level!

If you don't understand everything in a particular section while reading, don't worry! Financial issues are all interconnected, so what you don't understand in one section may be covered in another. My hope is that by the end of this book you will be able to step back and see your financial plan as a tool that can help you take your life where you want it to go!

For additional information and resources, including materials for course adoption, please visit personalfinanceforyoungprofessionals.com

Acknowledgments

Special thanks to London R., Brit Washburn, Verica Nakeva, Zach Kluver, and Scott D. for their invaluable feedback and discussions. Thank you to Bryan Pham and Catherine Nguyen for the cover design. Thank you to mom, dad, and Mooy for your unwavering support, and to everyone who encouraged me to turn what started as a mini guide into a book—and cheered me on along the entire way. Thank you to Joseph, Andres, and Catherine for your support and being amazing sounding boards. Lastly, thank you to Daisy for being the best dog in the world and keeping me company during the late nights that I spent writing. I could not have achieved this without you all.

Notes and Disclaimers

Note 1: All of the tax brackets, budgets, and assumptions in this book are based on "single" tax filing status in the year 2025 unless denoted otherwise.

Note 2: The inflation rate used in this text varies from 2.5% to 3%,[1] mostly because the true inflation rate is virtually impossible to calculate. Typically, inflation is calculated via the CPI (consumer price index) year over year growth, but the goods that are encompassed by the CPI regularly change, so it is not a true indicator of inflation experienced by the average person. Therefore, various sources report varying levels of inflation. For simplicity in this text, growth is offset by inflation via subtraction ([growth rate] − [inflation rate]). However, the mathematically correct way to incorporate inflation into your growth rates is to multiply ([1 + growth rate] × [1 − inflation rate]). In the first method, an 8% growth offset by a 2% inflation results in a 6% real growth. In the second method, the same scenario results in $(1 + 0.08) \times (1 − 0.02) = 5.84\%$. Since growth rates and inflation rates used for future projections are simply approximations based on history, using the first method has virtually no consequence in your calculations.

Note 3: All growth rates and interest percentages mentioned are annual unless specified otherwise.

Note 4: This book will not contain every detail or variation of each topic, but only the essentials plus a bit more. If it did contain everything, the book would be 10 times longer, 10 times more confusing, and 10 times more boring to read.

Disclaimer: I am not a licensed financial adviser or certified financial planner. The information presented in this book, while backed by reputable sources, is not professional financial advice and is for discussion and entertainment purposes only. You should do your own research before beginning any financial endeavor. The guidance contained in this book may not suit your specific personal financial needs.

CHAPTER 1

A Holistic View on Personal Finance

What Is Personal Finance?

Personal finance is exactly what it sounds like—personal and financial! It's all about creating a plan that works for YOU. In order to create the "best" plan, you must understand the theories and principles behind financial strategy. Understanding financial strategy will help you develop a plan that works for you and one that you will be able to implement consistently and change when necessary. Many people believe that there is a "best strategy" to achieve your financial goals, but in reality there are an infinite number of ways to reach your financial goals and still have a great balance in life. I will reiterate this again: There is not a single best way to achieve your financial goals. If anyone ever tells you that you must do XYZ to achieve ABC, then they are either full of bogus or they are trying to sell you something. Personal finance is all about creating a plan that not only works for your lifestyle, risk tolerance, and investment goals but also one that you fully understand so that you can adjust and adapt when changes in the economy, your job, life circumstances, or personal needs occur, as they inevitably will. You should understand how your decisions will impact your overall financial health and future so that you can make better choices!

The essence of personal finance is that beyond a certain income threshold, you will have the ability to save some amount of money and, more importantly, build wealth over time. Saving money is the basis of building wealth and developing a solid financial foundation. The saying *savings is the difference between your income and your ego* emphasizes the attitude required to build wealth. Every dollar spent above what is essential to survive is a luxury and can potentially be used for wealth-building activities. This is not to say that you should never treat yourself, but, rather, after a certain income level, saving is a choice. The money that you work hard for should be used for either wealth-building or to bring value in the form of the things you care most about. Moreover, what you do with the money that you're reserving for your future can make or break your financial health in terms of how you put it to work and how long it will take you to achieve your goals. After you lay out and follow a basic framework that works for you, everything that follows is optimization. You need to ensure that your money is going places where it will work the hardest for you AND where you will feel the most comfortable (i.e., not kept awake worrying at night).

Although a large piece of the personal finance puzzle, saving money for your future is not all there is to it. The primary purpose of personal finance is to allocate your money to places or things that will bring you and the people you love the most utility, whether in the present or the future.

Of additional importance is "F-U" money. This money is the amount of money you need to have in order to say F-U to the job that you're tired of and the boss who doesn't respect you or your personal time. Obviously, you can't do it if you're broke! Who's going to pay the bills? Jokes aside, the purpose of this money isn't necessarily about the job you hate or the boss you despise (I added that in for dramatic effect). It's about being able to live life on your own terms, not on your bank account's. Suppose you're so overwhelmed by the birth of your first child or adoption of your first dog that you want to take longer parental leave. Use your F-U money! Want to switch jobs and travel for 3 months between them? Use your F-U money! The point is not to be tied down to a job to such an extent that you absolutely need the next paycheck. Many people believe that the purpose of building a solid financial foundation is to retire early. While that may be the goal for certain individuals, the vast majority of us simply want financial security so we don't have to worry if we lose our job or need to take time off for physical or mental health reasons. The list of why someone may require F-U money is vast and cannot be covered in this guide, but when reading this section, surely something popped into your mind that you could use F-U money for. If nothing comes to mind immediately, let your imagination run wild!

Why Is This Relevant to Me? I'm So Young!

Consider the following two scenarios:

1. Jim is a 25-year-old recent college graduate who is earning $65k annually. He places $1k/month, or 18% of his gross salary, into an investment account until his target retirement age of 60 years old. At a historical inflation-adjusted average return of 8%, his $1k/month investment will grow to $2.1M, which will offer him a nice comfortable retirement even without a pension or social security. At a 4% annual withdrawal rate, Jim can withdraw $82k/year, which replaces his original salary with plenty of room to spare.

2. John is a 25-year-old recent college graduate who is also earning $65k annually. He lives as extravagantly as his salary will permit and spends all of his money without saving. "Saving is for old people!" he says. He waits until he is 35 to begin saving for retirement. Using the same $1k/month at 8% growth that Jim contributed, John will only have $877k by the time he turns 60, a paltry amount to retire on, and almost $1.2M less than Jim. For John to completely catch up with Jim in retirement savings, John will have to contribute $2,300/month until he turns 60! Do you think that suddenly beginning to save over $27k/year will be possible considering that 35-year-old John likely has a $438k home mortgage, two kids, two car payments, and a pet? Probably not. By the way, these are not exaggerations—these are U.S. averages.

The cost of waiting 10 years to begin investing is over $1,300 per month until retirement. We can see here that John still doesn't catch up with Jim even though he contributes more than double what Jim does from age 35 to 60 (Figure 1.1).

Don't worry if you didn't understand any of the numbers or terminology. The key takeaway is that the earlier you start saving, the less you have to worry about it in the future. The dollar that you save first will be the dollar that works the hardest for you. During a shareholder meeting in the late 1990s, Charlie Munger said, "The first $100,000 is a bitch, but you gotta do it." A little out of touch for the average American at the time,

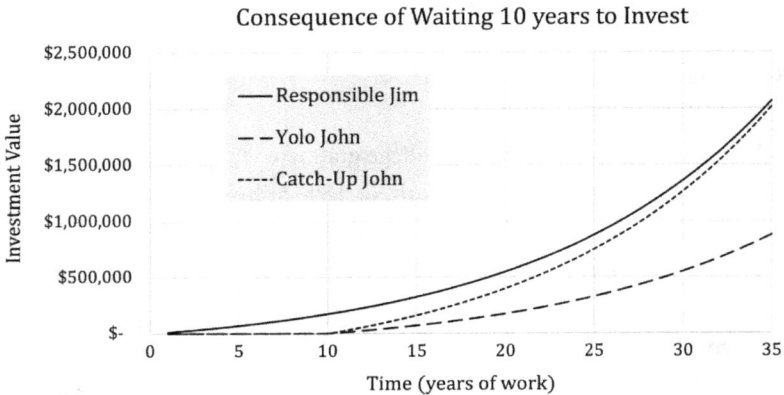

Figure 1.1 *Consequence of waiting 10 years to invest*

but quintessential advice nonetheless. The intention of his statement was to emphasize that your earliest investments will work the hardest for you and that the earlier you do it the better. A lump sum of $100k invested for the same duration and growth rate as Jim and John would be $1.07M and $542k, respectively. Notice that although Jim invested only 10 more years than John (35 vs. 25), the amount that he ended with would be more than double that of John.

You may be thinking, "I don't make enough money to be saving $1,000/month in my twenties," and that is completely okay. You can start saving with whatever amount you'd like. By learning about finances and saving any amount of money, you will have greater psychological awareness when you do start making enough to save something more substantial. Even if you can only save a few bucks a month now, you will begin exercising your "saving muscles." The last thing you want is to suddenly start making good money, not know what to do with it, and then make huge and costly mistakes. Start small and build your way up. You will make mistakes in your financial journey—it is a rite of passage and part of maturing financially. It is better to make mistakes when you have three or four digits in your accounts versus when there are six or seven digits. Understanding your psychological relationship with money and your financial risk tolerance are so important and should be developed *while* your earnings increase, not after. You absolutely do not need to wait until you make a lot of money to learn about finances or begin building wealth.

The Money Mindset

What Is Frugality?

Frugality: Careful management of material resources, especially money.

Frugality is spending less money on things that don't matter to you and spending more money on things that do. You will never achieve financial freedom if you must have the best of everything. Frugal people pick and choose where to spend their hard-earned money and spend less on things that don't matter as much to them. Being frugal does NOT mean being cheap. Frugality affects only you while being cheap affects others. David Allen said, "You can have anything you want, but not everything you want." Indulging in things that truly matter to you and making compromises on things that matter less is the essence of frugality.

If you absolutely love sushi and need to try every sushi restaurant in your city, go for it! If you love Star Wars and Legos, then go collect every Star Wars Lego set! However, you must be mindful and cut back on things that don't matter to you. Don't love cars? Drive a basic and reliable economy car. Don't care about fancy clothes? Buy cheap but high-quality clothes and don't buy into fashion trends.

Frugality is not buying the cheapest of everything to save money. Those types of purchases will often end up costing more money in the long run. Cheap things don't usually last long or deliver a great user experience. Frugality also doesn't mean not tipping public service workers, skimping on home and vehicle maintenance, or not paying friends back—that's just being cheap. Frugality is about being intentional in your allocation of capital to the things that require money in your life, not being cheap at the expense of those around you *or your future self.*

The Utility of Money

Money has utility in every part of your life. There is always something in your life that requires money, whether a new pair of shoes, a place to live, groceries, your car, charities, or even that pottery class you've been meaning to sign up for. All of these things are jostling for priority in your wallet, and you need to make the best decision as to what to spend your money on! Consider the following scenario:

It is a common belief that buying the best that you can afford is always the right choice—*buy nice or buy twice*. However, that doesn't always work in personal finance. You cannot afford the "nice" of everything! Suppose you must decide between buying a new pan for your kitchen (because you want to start cooking at home to save money) versus a new pair of work shoes. Buying nice for those can easily cost over $100 each. However, say you only have $150 to spend right now. While some might incur debt to buy the "nice" version of each, you choose to buy a less expensive pan so that you can afford nicer shoes without going into debt. After your less expensive pan wears out in a few years, you will have the money to purchase a nicer pan that hopefully will last a lot longer than the first. Perhaps you'll also learn a thing or two about caring for cookware along the way!

Although you did end up having to buy twice, you postponed the second purchase into the future so that your money today had utility elsewhere to improve your quality of life or build wealth instead of purchasing "subpar" $75 versions of each—or buying the "nice" of both and going into debt. This is just an example, but the idea holds true for many different scenarios in life, including purchasing experiences or having to make a choice between multiple items. This concept of making decisions with limited resources is the foundation of economics and is a psychological science as much as it is a mathematical one.

This debate can be made with any two decisions regarding money and time:

- Investing in the stock market versus spending the extra money on higher quality construction materials for a home renovation project
- Spending more money on a better education versus putting the money toward starting a business
- Spending 2 hours every weekend mowing your lawn with your own equipment that you purchased for $1,500, or paying someone $100 every 1 to 2 weeks to do it
- Spending more money on a newer car in hopes of reducing maintenance costs down the road versus saving money on a used car

and putting the extra money toward job training that will increase
your income

- Going on three domestic trips in the United States or going on
  one trip abroad
- Eating at a mid-priced restaurant twice a week or going out to a
  fancy place twice a month

The list goes on!

It may be challenging or unproductive to pinpoint exactly where the
breakeven point is, but factoring in your happiness (in economics they
refer to this metric as *utils*) can help you make decisions. To add greater
complexity, all of the aforementioned choices have points of diminishing
returns. This point will be different for everyone, but the concept is that
beyond a certain point, adding "stuff" will not make you any happier than
you already are. Consider the following example:

> You are craving ice cream, so you go out to a local ice cream shop
> where they are running a promotion. If you can correctly answer
> a question about personal finance, you are entitled to a free ice
> cream. Amazing! Because you are reading this book, you answer
> correctly and get your free ice cream. You are extremely happy
> with this outcome and decide to answer another question to get
> another free ice cream. After all, you didn't learn all about personal
> finance for just one serving. While eating your second ice cream,
> you are happy, but you aren't as happy as you were with the first
> ice cream. After you finish your second ice cream, you go for a
> third, but later realize that it might have been a mistake as you
> are now feeling sick. You have reached the point of diminishing
> returns! An additional ice cream has very little positive impact on
> your happiness. In fact, it has actually had a negative impact!

In most situations, the point of diminishing returns is more challenging
to pinpoint than in the aforementioned example, but the concept is still
the same. The idea is that placing additional resources into an activity
doesn't guarantee a greater amount of *utils*. The utility of money is always
changing based on the status of your life and will continue to be dynamic

as your life becomes more complex. Understanding that your money is a limited resource that can bring *utils* into your life and the necessity of deploying that money skillfully is the essence of the concept of the utility of money.

Opportunity Cost

If you've ever had to forgo something to pursue something else, then you understand the concept of opportunity cost. It is the value of what you forgo when you choose one option over another. For example, you have $1,000 to invest into a fund that returns 10% annually, but your little cousin asks you instead to invest $1,000 into his lemonade stand that will only produce 6% annual returns. You, being the nice cousin that you are, choose to support your cousin's lemonade stand. You are doing great by making a 6% return on your investment; however, you are actually incurring an opportunity cost of 4% by not pursuing the original 10% option. Naturally, there are different risks, liquidity (your accessibility to money), and other implications associated with each of these choices, which is why it's not always perfectly clear which is the best investment. The key to understanding opportunity cost is to think about what the best alternative to what you are currently doing is and about the differences in value of the available options.

Another example is that you make $15/hour translating children's books online. You can work remotely wherever and whenever you want. You had planned to work for 2 hours one evening when your friend invited you to the pub for a drink. You decide not to work and instead go out and spend $20 on drinks. Not only did you spend $20 on drinks, but you also gave up $30 in income since you didn't work. In this case, your total cost of getting drinks with your friends is $20 actual cost + $30 opportunity cost = $50. This doesn't necessarily mean that you lost $50 in this transaction; it simply means that you gave up $30 in addition to spending $20 on drinks. You have to decide if the interaction was worth $20 in addition to the alternative of spending the evening working and earning $30.

This can work in the absence of money too. You were supposed to get drinks with a friend, but you're stuck in the office working on a last-minute request for a report that your boss needs by tomorrow at 8 a.m. The opportunity cost of your complete report is a great night out with friends, which you unfortunately cannot bill your boss for—what was I saying about F-U money earlier?

It is not practical to spend every hour of your day working even if it is best from an opportunity-cost standpoint. You can have a healthy work–life balance despite the seemingly high opportunity cost of everything in life. How you can go about this is by setting a number of hours for work, personal, and social time each week. After those predetermined hours (and maybe some wiggle room), you can begin calculating opportunity costs for what your time is worth.

Not only are your life activities going to constantly vie for your financial and temporal resources, but there may also be investment choices that you need to make that require you to deploy an opportunity-cost mindset. Should you invest in the stock market or purchase investment properties? Aside from personal preference and the stochastic nature of investing and finances, the opportunity cost can usually be calculated.

Your Money Mindset

Many people have a negative mindset on money overall. This may be the result of the way they were raised, the current economic or political state, or their current financial situation. Whatever the reason, the mindset with which you approach personal finance will become the foundation for how you will manage your financial health going forward. Imagine wanting to lose a few pounds and get into better shape and the only thing you can think about is "I will never be better because it's the way I am and the way my parents and ancestors were." To be clear, I am not discrediting the difficulty of achieving something very challenging. The obstacles in every individual's journey will be of various shapes and sizes. The idea is that many people believe they cannot change when they actually can with the right attitude, mindset, and tools. Change will not happen overnight, but it will happen over time if you are consistent and intentional.

People don't take action on things related to their personal finances because it's much easier to say "The economy and job market sucks because of the current president" or "I have so much student debt because financial aid screwed me over" or "I'm stuck in this expensive car payment because the dealership misled me," instead of getting up and doing something about it. It's much easier to stay on the couch and say, "I will always be out of shape," than it is to get up and go for a walk. In the short run, it's easier to make excuses regarding your financial health, but, in the long run, it's much harder to be poor. It is imperative not to become a victim of a negative attitude about your personal finances. You can control how much you make; you can control how much you keep; you can control how much you spend. There are so many more financial options at your disposal than most people think. One of the primary purposes of this book is to give you both perspective and knowledge about the choices available to you pertaining to personal finance and how they can impact you. You should strive to control what you can control and understand what tools you have at your disposal to react when things happen that are out of your control.

The Time Value of Money

The value of your money will change over time. It may increase if invested properly or decrease due to depreciation or inflation. Your money has a certain buying power today, but over time that buying power is eroded by inflation. In general, inflation occurs when the supply of money is larger than the supply of goods and services. When there is a limited amount of goods and services and excess money to purchase them, prices go up. Despite how people feel about inflation, a small amount is indicative of a healthy economy. Inflation indicates that people, in general, have more money to spend. In a deflationary economy, people have less money, so prices go down. Historically, the only periods in which the prices of goods and services fell were in periods of recession and depression. You need to consider inflation for your financial calculations. A $100 bill today buys less than it did 20 years ago and will buy even less 20 years from now.

The overall inflation rate since 1958 is 3.7%; however, from 1974 to 1982, the United States experienced a period of very high inflation of 8.6% that skewed the average higher than what occurred for the 40 years following. During this period, certain economic policies drove inflation to be outrageously high. The details will not be discussed in this book, but if those outlier years are removed from the data set, the average inflation for the remaining 58 years is 2.9%. Inflation over the past 30 years is 2.4%. While a few percentage points might not seem like a lot, inflation compounded over several decades can lead to quite a significant decrease in purchasing power.

On the other hand, investing your money properly can do exactly the opposite of eroding purchasing power. If you invest and generate a return that is higher than the rate of inflation, the future value of your money will have more buying power than it does today! If you can outpace inflation, then you will be rewarded in the future with greater buying power.

In the next section and in the "Financial Formulas" Section in the appendix, we will cover some basic financial calculations that will help you wrap your head around what exactly a decrease or increase in buying power means mathematically. If you don't care for the math, all you need to know is that inflation causes your money to decrease in value over time. A dollar today is worth more than a dollar in the future, and investing your money at a rate that is higher than the rate of inflation can help you have greater purchasing power down the line.

The Eighth Wonder: Compound Interest

Compound interest is often referred to as the eighth wonder of the world. It is extremely powerful and, when utilized correctly, can help bring your wealth to a whole different dimension. Why is that? While simple interest pays you the same amount in each pay period, compounding interest takes the previous payment and adds it to your total investment and pays you interest based on the new value. For math nerds, this is known as exponential growth, and the equation is as follows:

$$[FV]=[PV] \cdot (1+\frac{r}{n})^{nt}$$

where [FV] is future value, [PV] is present value, r is the rate of return as a decimal, n is the number of compounding periods in the year, and t is the number of years.

Consider the following cases:

Case A: $10,000 initial investment at 10% simple interest. Annu-ally, the payout is $1,000 ($10,000 × 0.10). After 20 years, the total amount is $30,000. Not too shabby!

Case B: $10,000 initial investment at 10% interest compounded annually. For the first year, the payout is the same as Case A: $1,000. However, the $1,000 is added back to the principal and the next year you are paid 10% of $11,000, meaning your payment is $1,100, which is $100 more than it was last year! Continue this pattern for 20 years and your total amount is $67,275—a value that is significantly higher than in Case A!

The aforementioned cases serve as simple examples of the beauty of com-pounding interest. Let's look at the ending value for a longer time period: 40 years.

Case A: $50,000
Case B: $452,593 (this is not a typo)

In the first 10 years, there isn't a huge difference in simple versus com-pound interest. However, in the long run, compound interest dominates simple interest because compound interest is growth on top of growth rather than growth on the initial contribution only (Figure 1.2).

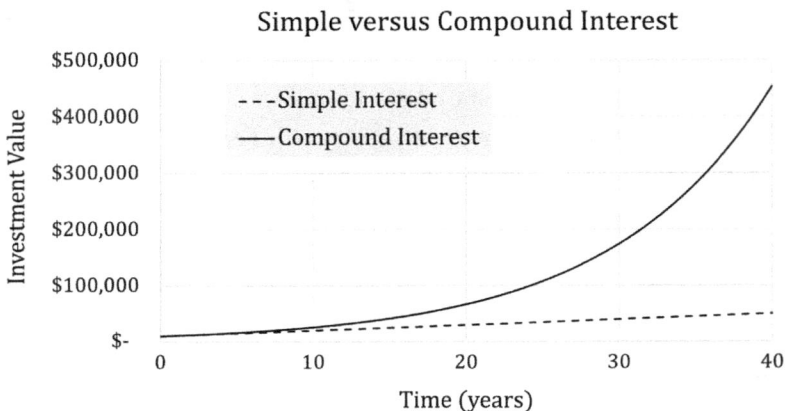

Figure 1.2 Simple versus compound interest

Keep in mind that this is compounding over 40 years with **no additional contribution** other than the $10,000 initial investment. If a 10% rate of return seems unrealistic to you, consider that the S&P 500 has returned 11.88% annually since its modern inception in 1957. (It has actually been around since 1926 when it had 233 stocks vs. roughly 500 today.)

If these numbers and definitions make your head spin, don't worry! Most of the nifty formulas used earlier and laid out in the following are put into a simple interface here.[2] The key takeaway from this section is that you want to take advantage of compound interest as early as possible in your life so that it has time to work its magic. In the same vein that you want compound interest to help you, you also don't want compound interest to work against you in the form of debt.

Examples of Financial Calculations

All things finance-related come down to mathematics, and the possibilities of what you can calculate are endless. There is no magic involved, even though it might seem like it. Understanding the extent to which a financial choice will affect you is the reason why you should know what you can and cannot calculate. (Spoiler, you can pretty much calculate everything.) There are certain things such as market rate of return and inflation that are based on chance, but you can utilize ranges and use those numbers in concrete financial calculations, which will act as edge cases in your analyses. Here are some examples of common financial calculations that use the formulas in the "Financial Formulas" section in the appendix:

- Figure out how much you need to save annually to retire comfortably.
- Calculate how much you need to save each month so you can buy a house in a certain number of years.
- Calculate how much you have to invest at 8% growth to have $50,000 saved for your child's college fund for when they turn 18.
- See how much your car will depreciate in dollars if it reduces in value by 15% each year for 10 years.

- Figure out the impact of maxing out your Roth IRA (independent retirement arrangement) each year for 30 years.
- Calculate whether or not you should consider working at a company with a pension versus company stock versus 401(k).
- Calculate how much interest you will pay on a loan balance in the first year of car or homeownership.
- Calculate the growth potential of $1,000 invested in the stock market at 8% versus using it to buy a lawnmower and saving $50 a week.
- Adjust $30,000 in today's dollars to account for 2.5% inflation for 20 years.
- See if you're saving enough if the market returns 6% instead of the historical 10%, and see how many more years you would have to work if that does happen.

The possibilities of what you can calculate are endless. In the beginning, it may seem overwhelming to perform all these calculations. Luckily, there are plenty of online calculators available to help you! Whether you use an online calculator or do them yourself, be sure to start out using numbers that you're sure of so you know the result of your equation is perfect. Compound interest is a very funny thing, and most people have no intuition about it. Consider the growth of $50 a month from birth until death, an average of approximately 70 years, at the S&P 500 historical growth rate of 11.88%. Your intuition might say that you may amass around $1M or perhaps even $2M—a decent chunk of cash for a measly $50/month investment! The actual result is a staggering $13.7M. Of course, it is wise to build conservatism into your calculations, but don't be surprised when the numbers are much larger or smaller than you think!

What Is an Investment?

An investment is a resource that you put away now to utilize in the future. Whether it be time spent learning a skill or craft (investing in yourself so you can earn a higher salary), seeds that you plant and water for months (so you can eat in the future), or money (that you hope will grow enough to support you when you are too old to work). The focus of this book is, as you may have guessed, financial investments, which many people generalize as only "stocks." While a stock is a popular vehicle of investment, it is not the only form! A financial investment is a place where you set your money and give it an opportunity to generate a return to be collected in the future. There are many types of investments: stocks, bonds, mutual funds, index funds, businesses, real estate, and so on. The type of investments you choose to have in your portfolio should reflect your risk tolerance, desired level of return, and involvement. For example, someone who has no interest in managing anything should not invest in real estate because it is a very hands-on investment despite what the "TikTok Gurus" tend to say.

Another way to look at investments is to view them as paying your future self. You are taking money or resources away from your current self in hopes that your future self will benefit from your investment. On the contrary, debt is stealing from your future self to pay your current self. More on that later!

The Basic Principles of Financial Security

At this point, you may have decided whether or not you want to read this entire book. I won't be insulted if you don't. In reality, you only need the following simple principles that will virtually guarantee financial success if applied consistently and methodically:

1. Avoid consumer debt.
2. Earn more than you spend.
3. Pocket the difference.
4. Invest in diversified, low-cost index funds in tax-advantaged accounts.

These rules will form the basis for all our discussions in this book. There are many nuances, formalities, optimizations, and tricks to chat about. Despite the numerous paths you can take, your personal finance journey doesn't need to be complicated. It can be as simple as automating everything and leaving it alone, checking it once or twice a year, and tweaking it every time you have a notable life event (having a kid, getting a big promotion, getting married, selling/buying a house, etc.). As long as you implement these rules consistently in your personal finance strategy, any modification to your method is simply an optimization and not a change in overall financial philosophy!

Why Are You Writing This Book?

Raise your hand if you've been told any of the following:

- "It's rude to ask people about their salary."
- "It's rude to ask them how much that costs."
- "It's rude to ask someone whether they took out a loan to buy that item."
- "I will need to work until I die."
- "I can't afford to take time off to be with my family during the holidays."
- *proudly* "I'm not good with finances."
- "I can't do anything until my next paycheck comes in."
- "I can't afford to take time off even when I'm sick."
- "I'll be in debt for the next 10+ years."

Finance is often perceived as a taboo subject, and I wonder how hard it is for people to pretend that money doesn't make the world go round! The result of this is that our youth will grow up never being exposed to any of this. Thus, many young adults go into the real world not knowing anything about financial management and eventually make huge mistakes that will set them back years. Even parents or relatives with the best intentions may give poor advice based on what they learned when they were growing up. Without a solid understanding of where the advice came from and the math behind it, it is challenging to understand what to actually do with it and how it impacts you, which brings us back to that decades-long game of telephone! Beyond a certain point of income, becoming financially educated is more important than earning a higher salary. There are plenty of people out there who earn over $250k annually and are two paychecks away from foreclosing on their home and are forced to work until they drop dead. There are also plenty of people out there who make $75k/year who retire comfortably as millionaires. Make no mistake; the Person A making $75k/year with $150k in investments is doing far better in life than the Person B making $250k/year with the same $150k. Think of it like this: $150k in savings buys Person A 2 full years of freedom while Person B cannot even survive 8 months without a job.

This book is here to help you to be in control of your finances to whatever extent you want to be. If you learn how to be financially responsible and still choose to make objectively bad decisions with your money because they truly bring you happiness and fulfillment, then more power to you! As long as you understand the consequences, you are always welcome to exercise the "personal" part of personal finance.

Scott's Thoughts: The "Personal" Part of Personal Finance

While I will remain as objective as possible throughout this book and adhere to historically proven and mathematically optimal financial strategies, I want to take some time to describe my personal money management philosophy and strategy **as it pertains to my life**. Keep in mind that this is my personal strategy and is not financial advice (technically no part of this book is financial advice). My financial strategy stems from my psychological relationship with money as yours will for you. In each of these boxes, I will describe my philosophy as well as the reasoning if it differs from the standard rules.

About Me

I grew up middle class. The kind of middle class where you took a family road trip once a year, had economy cars in the driveway, did activities like piano and gymnastics lessons for me and my sister, and lived in a regular house in the suburbs (without the white picket fence). We were also the kind of middle class that did cheaper activities—camping (before it got gentrified), always cooking at home (McDonalds was a treat if we got A's on our report cards), fixing our own cars and mowing our own lawns, and using sliced white bread for our cheeseburgers and hot dogs instead of costlier buns. Like many American middle-class families, our financial security was constantly threatened by minor upsets, and, due to a lack of financial education and foundation, we were always one event away from disaster. It was nobody's fault—the way you were taught to view money has a monumental impact on your financial perspective, and it's nearly impossible to know what's right and wrong when you don't know what you don't know.

My background is in engineering. I hold Bachelor and Master of Science degrees in Mechanical Engineering, with a minor in Mathematics, and 5 years of industry experience. In addition, I have over 12 years of math tutoring experience with various applications, including financial mathematics and economics. I teach my students how to be first-principle thinkers and apply fundamental concepts to solve complicated problems. *Personal Finance for Young Professionals* utilizes my ability to teach hard topics to people in ways they can understand. The technical aspects of this text are largely in keeping with received opinion in the industry, but are broken down into digestible, bite-sized pieces that can easily be understood by anyone with a background in basic high school math.

After entering the real world and earning my first paycheck, I realized that I would need to learn how to manage my money on my own. I did not want to rely on someone else to do that for the rest of my life. What if that person retires or isn't around anymore? What if they don't understand my financial needs as well as I do or what if those needs shift over time? Most importantly, it costs money to have someone manage your finances—way more money than you think. Through a combination of focused research, daily immersion in personal finance content, conversations with other finance nerds like myself, and good ol' trial and error, I not only learned about tools and strategies that can be used to take control of and be successful with your finances but also learned about the psychology required to understand your relationship with money and the relevant decisions you make.

I have spent years discussing finance with colleagues, friends, and family. I am constantly being asked questions about what to do and how and when to do it. As a result, I decided to dedicate time and energy to putting together a comprehensive book that any young professional can use to get their footing in personal finance. While this book would be appropriate for anyone who is interested in learning personal finance, young professionals will benefit the most. I will give you essential knowledge so that you know which knobs to turn to steer your financial boat in the direction you want it to go. I hope you enjoy!

CHAPTER 2

The Flow of Personal Finance

There is a mathematically ideal process to maximize your wealth-building capabilities, and it is generalized by the Personal Finance Flowchart. It is an elegant way to move quickly and efficiently toward your financial goals with only a few key decisions. It represents the optimal strategy and priorities you should focus on to maximize your finances and is backed by mathematics and the current tax code.

If you don't understand everything now, don't worry. This book contains everything you need to follow these steps:

0. Create a budget, reduce expenses, and set realistic goals.
1. Build an emergency fund.
2. Get employer-sponsored matching funds.
3. Pay down high- and moderate-interest debt.
4. Save for retirement in an IRA.
5. Save more for retirement in tax-advantaged space.
6. Pay off low-interest debt, save for other goals, and invest in non–tax-advantaged accounts.

The Personal Finance Flowchart

Step 0: Create a Budget, Reduce Expenses, and Set Realistic Goals

The first step to building a solid financial foundation is making a budget, and the most critical part of that is being realistic about it. A simple and realistic budget that you follow is far better than a budget that is complicated and overly ambitious.

You need to be realistic about what expenses you can reduce. You don't want to budget $40/week for food and realize that you have to spend at least $75/week to eat healthfully. Aim for the heavy hitters like rent and transportation before going after smaller ones like Netflix, Spotify, or your gym membership. Reducing one large expense is generally easier than trying to minimize multiple smaller expenses.

Step 1: Build an Emergency Fund

A typical emergency fund (or E-fund) contains between 3 and 6 months of essential expenses and serves as a tool to avoid debt in a financial emergency. To find this number, consider every essential expense you have in a month and multiply by the number of months you want to have in reserve. This number has a wide range because people's living situations differ greatly. If you live with your parents and work a low-risk job, you may be able to get away with a 3-month reserve. If you have a job that has a lot of uncertainty, you may want to consider a 6-month emergency fund. If you are supporting a family on a single income, you may even want to consider having a year or more of reserve cash. The purpose of the emergency fund is for, well, emergencies. While the size of the emergency fund is based on one of the largest unexpected expenses you'll face—job loss—it also covers day-to-day emergencies such as medical emergencies, unexpected car problems or home repairs, and so on. Your typical emergency will not utilize the entire emergency fund. The average emergency in the United States is approximately $1,400 to $1,700.[3] If you have trouble gathering an emergency fund now, consider gathering just enough cash to cover your insurance deductibles. What is *not* an emergency is that nice Gucci bag that just went on sale or that new 300-quart Yeti cooler. Place your emergency fund into an FDIC-insured high-yield savings account and don't look at it! While the 3-to-6-month emergency fund is a great rule of thumb, it is important to consider your personal situation. For example, while one person has a 6-month emergency fund, another person might consider having a 3-month emergency fund but with an extra $10k set aside because their home is old and prone to needing emergency repair. You may even want to include nonessential expenses in your emergency fund calculations so you do not have to alter your lifestyle if you lose your job.

It can be daunting to build your cash reserve if you aren't able to save a ton each month, but luckily it does not have to happen all at once. If your goal is to have a 6-month fund, you can save in tiers. You might save 1 month first, then divert a portion of your monthly cash savings to Step 2. Once you reach 2 to 3 months of reserves, you might divert a portion of your cash to Step 3. Now you can slowly build up to your 6-month target. As mentioned, most emergencies will not utilize your entire emergency fund, so it is ok to slowly build this up over time. Every dollar you add to your emergency fund will improve your financial security! If done strategically, Steps 1, 2, and 3 of the flowchart can be done simultaneously.

Scott's Thoughts: Emergency Fund Amount

The typical rule of thumb for cash on hand is anywhere between 3 and 6 months of expenses, which is adjusted based on your risk tolerance. I typically consider myself a risk-taker and am tolerant to job loss since I have multiple sources of income. Theoretically, I should be comfortable with about 3 months of cash (about $10k for core living expenses and $15k including nonessentials). However, in the times that I have had that amount of cash on hand, I felt inadequately prepared for a real crisis. I prefer to have over 6 months of cash and an additional buffer should a large home-repair item arise. My comfortable number is around $50k, that is, just enough cash to start feeling uncomfortable about having too much cash.

Consider that while an emergency fund is intended to de-risk your financial system, real risk is what you cannot plan for. Your emergency fund is expected to cover the largest *predictable* emergency, but the actual largest emergency is unknown.

Where my philosophy differs is that I am willing to use a portion of my cash on hand for investments if the right opportunity arises. For example, I prefer to keep around $50k in cash, but am willing to use up to $25k of it toward an investment property, leaving me with $25k leftover as a core emergency fund, which I will build back as quickly as possible. At the end of the day, purchasing an investment property is not truly a purchase but a transfer of an asset from cash to real estate.

Step 2: Employer-Sponsored Matching Funds

If your employer offers any sort of match for a retirement account like a 401(k), 403(b), or similar, absolutely take advantage of that prior to other investments. Matches are typically 1:1 or 2:1 contribution, meaning for every dollar you put in, your employer puts in a dollar or 50 cents—a guaranteed 100% or 50% return, respectively. You will not find a guaranteed return like this on any other kind of investment.

The nuances of these tax-advantaged accounts will be discussed in detail later. Some companies require mandatory participation in their retirement savings programs, which isn't at all a bad thing. They vary from industry to industry and carry different policies, rules, and limits. It is best to research the specific type of account your employer offers and its rules so you can optimize your strategy.

Step 3: Pay Down High- and Moderate-Interest Debt

Paying off debt is essentially a guaranteed return of whatever the interest rate is. The logic is that you no longer have to pay interest on the debt that you paid off, so you are getting money back into your pocket. The general threshold for this amount is 5% (except for mortgages). Any interest above 5% should be paid off sooner rather than later, and rates over 7% to 8% should be paid off immediately. If your rate is in the double digits, that is a pants-on-fire emergency that you need to take care of at all costs! Some people consider 6% to be the threshold for paying off debt, especially in a higher interest rate environment. See Section "Why Is 5% the Threshold for Paying Off Debt Versus Investing" in the appendix for the analysis behind the 5% threshold for debt payoff.

Step 4: Savings for Retirement in an IRA

The next step is to begin utilizing more of your tax-advantaged space, namely the Roth IRA,[4] which will be discussed in detail later. The maximum contribution to any IRA is $7,000 in 2025 and gets adjusted for inflation every so often.

Step 5: Save More for Retirement

This step is maxing out your 401(k) (or comparable plan) up to the IRS (Internal Revenue Service) maximum ($23,500 per person in 2025). This will essentially max out your tax-advantaged space for conventional and commonly available retirement accounts.

If you complete Step 5, which includes maxing out your Roth IRA and 401(k) or equivalent, you will be contributing $30,500/year to your retirement accounts. If you project that forward for 30 years (age 30–60) at a growth rate of 8% (historical S&P 500 return of 11.9% minus 3.8% inflation[5] and rounded down for conservatism), you will end up with $3.46M in today's spending power. Work the full 40 years (25–65) and it will be $7.90M, not including your employer match. Note that contribution limits typically go up following the inflation rate and have already been taken into account; however, your salary (and subsequently your employer match) will likely outpace inflation throughout your career, so the $7.90M figure is actually quite conservative. This figure also does not include any other assets that you might accumulate over the years either.

If this is "all you can do," you are already light years ahead of most.

Step 6: Save for Other Goals and Investment Optimization

In the last step, you can begin saving for other things such as a home, vacations, weddings, new cars, and so on. At this point, you may have extra cash to invest or pay off low-interest debt that is below a 5% interest rate. While it is important to optimize your investment strategy, it is simply an *optimization*. The fact that you are saving at this level puts you miles ahead of the average person. As long as you are hitting your personal savings target(s) and properly utilizing your tax-advantaged space, everything after that is simply fine-tuning!

Note that between 1959 and 2022, the average American has saved only 8.96%[6] of their paycheck. You should save at least 15% of your paycheck as a baseline if you plan on working until retirement age, and more if you want to retire early. It is common to see 20% as the recommended saving value: 15% toward investments and 5% as cash for large purchases.

When (Not) to Take Financial Advice

At some point in your life, you have been given financial advice, whether from a parent, an older relative, a friend, or acquaintance. You may have received financial advice from someone whom you trust and with whom you have a great relationship. You may have received financial advice from someone who seems well-off, and that person may very well be looking out for your best interests. However, all these things don't mean that their financial advice is sound. Maybe you've followed someone's recommendation in the past and ended up in a pickle because of it, realizing too late that the advice you thought was good was actually bogus. You may have received advice such as the following:

1. "You should finance a car to build your credit."
2. "You should buy XYZ stock because it's going to triple in value."
3. "Your 401(k) is a scam because you don't own it."
4. "XYZ cryptocurrency is going to the moon."
5. "The safest place for your money is physical cash (under your mattress)."
6. "You should buy a home to build equity."
7. "You should buy a brand-new car to not have to pay for maintenance."
8. "Retirement accounts are bad because they lock your money away until you're 60 years old."
9. "You should buy a home for the tax deduction."

The aforementioned statements are bogus for the following reasons:

1. You can build credit without paying double-digit interest rates, which will happen if it's your first big loan as a young adult with no credit. Using a credit card for small expenses and paying it off each month will be perfectly adequate for building credit.
2. Nobody can predict the stock market, not even Warren Buffet, Peter Lynch, or Michael Burry (he predicted the 2008 crash and was right only once).
3. Your 401(k) contributions are held in a managed brokerage account, just as the money you put in the bank gets held and

tracked digitally by the bank and not in a little box with your name on it.

4. Purely speculative investments are also known as gambling.

5. FDIC-insured banks versus cash under your mattress hmm…

6. Exchanging a lower rent payment for a mortgage with maintenance costs solely for the purpose of "building equity" is almost always a losing game. Notice how the people who suggest this have most of their net worth tied up in home equity and have very few actual investments. Buying a primary residence is a personal preference and lifestyle choice, not an investment.

7. New cars depreciate at a far greater rate than almost any used car's maintenance will cost you (sans major repairs like engine or transmission replacement).

8. You get huge tax breaks as a reward for using tax-advantaged retirement accounts. There are many ways to retrieve this money preretirement.

9. While it is true that certain home expenses are tax deductible, the value of those deductions must exceed the standard deduction. More so, it is foolish to spend money to save money. Keep in mind you only save on taxes via a deduction, not as a tax credit. In other words, at the 24% tax bracket, a $10,000 deduction will only save you $2,400 in taxes, not $10,000.

In addition to being able to spot bad financial advice, you should be able to spot when not to listen to people outright. Here are some examples of the types of people who are bad with finances:

- The person is not wealthy or "living very comfortably." End of statement. Why would you take financial advice from someone who isn't wealthy? Would you take home-buying advice from a homeless person? If their advice was so good, they would be wealthy. Do not confuse "having nice things" with "comfortable"— many people have nice things but can't actually afford them.

- The person has a lot of things but not a lot of investments or freedom. Got a sick car/boat/house/toy but living paycheck to paycheck? It means they went broke trying to look rich.

- They can't tell you how much they spend or save in a year. I once had some folks ask me for financial advice on what to do with some lump sum of money. The first thing I asked them was how much they spend in a year to determine if their emergency fund was adequate. They couldn't tell me an answer to the nearest $100k.
- They have credit card debt or other high-interest or unsecured debt such as personal loans. The double-digit interest rate incurred on a credit card is crippling.
- They tell you if the stock market, or any market (real estate, interest rates, etc.), is going to go up or down. This one drives me insane. If they were so sure of the market going up or down, they would put their money where their mouth is and easily become a billionaire! However, they are not a billionaire because they don't actually know. In fact, they don't even know with 50.1% certainty because if they did, statistically they would beat the market. Winning $100 with a 50.1% success rate and losing $100 with a 49.9% failure rate is statistical win: $+\$100 \times 0.501 - \$100 \times 0.499 = +\$0.20$. Scale up a few orders of magnitude for a few months and you'll easily become a billionaire! (That was sarcasm by the way.) I always respond to these comments by saying, "If you're so sure about the market going up/down then why don't you put your house and life savings on it? You will easily be able to tenfold your money in a few months and retire with millions!"
- They make purely emotional or impulsive decisions with their money instead of objectively thinking about the utility that it could bring them.
- If any person has made any of the aforementioned statements 1 through 9, it automatically disqualifies them from being a reliable source of financial information.

Note that the aforementioned traits have nothing to do with their actual character. There is no correlation between their financial status or education and their quality as a person. The point is to discourage you from taking financial advice from certain people in order to avoid getting yourself stuck in situations similar to those described. If anything, take

---

Beware: Multilevel Marketing Schemes

Multilevel Marketing Schemes (MLMs), also known as pyramid schemes, are scams that involve getting people to believe that they are business owners. The victims are forced to buy the products that they are trying to sell and then are asked to recruit other people to do the same thing in order to make their quota. Other characteristics of MLMs are pushy sales tactics by people who can't quite tell you how much money they make in the job. They have *upline* people who essentially make money by recruiting other people to the scheme, hence the name multilevel.

Rather than getting scammed by random people, many people who get sucked into MLMs are sucked in by friends and family, since you need to have the connection in order to make the sale or get someone to join the scheme.

Many people who work for MLMs are genuinely good people who didn't know better, and they unfortunately rarely make money. Usually, they lose money in pursuit of promised financial freedom and business ownership. In general, if a job sounds too good to be true, it probably is.

---

their advice with a grain of salt (or an entire saltshaker). Wealth is often generational. People who come from poor families are likely to remain poor. It takes years or generations to climb out of poverty, and poor financial information just makes it that much harder. A great place to start is to become financially literate—it costs nothing to go on Google and learn about finances. Even purchasing this book is inexpensive compared with making financial mistakes that can affect your generation and future generations.

On the contrary, here are some things to look for that indicate people are *good* with their finances:

- They have multiple sources of income (e.g., investment properties, businesses, etc.).
- They are not worried about job loss (i.e., they have adequate emergency fund and are financially independent from their work).

- They are sensible with their purchases and live within their means. Having expensive stuff does not necessarily mean that someone is not financially sensible. It's all relative. A $750k home on a $300k income is sensible, while a $400k home on a $70k income is not. A $100k car is sensible on a $300k income, but a $50k car on a $75k income is not.
- They teach their kids about finances rather than simply giving them money.
- They live modestly but have a lot of time to do the things they love.
- They have no debt (perhaps aside from a mortgage).
- They retired before traditional age and are living comfortably.
- They don't make impulsive purchases; that is, they think through every purchase thoroughly and really consider the value that something is going to bring.
- They don't panic when market corrections or crashes occur because their investment strategy is rock solid.

CHAPTER 3

Building a Solid Budget

Using a budget does not mean that you are broke or that you have to restrict yourself—this is a huge misconception. A budget gives you the power to direct your hard-earned money where you want it to go! You work hard for your money, so why shouldn't you get to decide where every dollar goes? Without a budget, you are letting your urges and intuition determine where your money goes. Having a structure for how you allocate money will help you reach your financial goals while being able to quantify how much you value each aspect of the things in life that cost you money. Having a budget allows you to allocate more dollars to the things that matter the most to you!

You might be thinking that you rarely overspend and, therefore, you don't need a budget. Even if you are a modest spender and have lots of money left over in your bank account at the end of each month, you probably aren't immediately putting that money in places where it will work the hardest for you. Having a budget will allow you to place your money where you want to ahead of time and let it start working for you immediately without you having to think about what to do with it. Every dollar that you earn should be allocated to either build wealth or improve your lifestyle, and a budget is going to help you do exactly that.

Step-by-Step Budgeting

Summary:

- Step 1: Track or backtrack your spending for 3 to 6 months; 1 year is ideal to get historical data and remove any seasonal variability.
- Step 2: Understand basic budgeting principles and rules of thumb.

- Step 3: Use rules as guidelines to develop a budget that you are happy with.
- Step 4: Continue to track spending.
- Step 5: Tweak your budget as you gain more insight on your spending habits and needs.

Let's take a deeper dive into the steps:

Step 1: Track your spending for 3 to 6 months, ideally for a year or more to get historical data and understand your seasonal variability.

This step is absolutely crucial to building your budget. Most people know approximately how much they spend each month but rarely know what everything is going toward. How many times have you looked at your credit card statement and wondered, "How the heck did I spend all that money?" This part simply helps you understand where you're at so you can set realistic and attainable goals.

Your tracking spreadsheet does not need to be complicated. The only data you truly need is the category and how much it costs. Data that would be nice to have is the item purchased along with the date (just the month will suffice). You should be able to look back on banking and credit card statements to gather this data. A typical expense tracker is shown in Figure 3.1.

There may be another section in your sheet to track to totals of each subcategory (Figure 3.2).

A free template for this spreadsheet with instructions as to how to use is located at: personalfinanceforyoungprofessionals.com.

From here, you can see what percentage of your income goes to each category. This will give you a baseline of what you need to adjust in order to make a balanced budget that works for you.

Trans. Date	Description	Subcategory	Credit	Account
1/2/2021	Walmart (examples)	Shopping	$145.96	Discover Credi
1/5/2021	Amazon return	Shopping	-$30.00	Chase Credit
1/9/2021	Mcdonalds	Food & Drink	$56.28	Chase Credit
1/15/2021	Centerpoint Gas Company	Utilities	$10.00	Discover Credi

Figure 3.1 Budget expense tracker sample (1/2)

Categories	Subcategory	Jan	Feb
		1	2
Essential	Car	$0	$0
Essential	Gas	$0	$0
Essential	Utilities	$10	$0
Essential	Groceries	$0	$0
Lifestyle	Food & Drink	$56	$0
Lifestyle	Travel	$0	$0
Lifestyle	Shopping	$116	$0
Lifestyle	Entertainment	$0	$0
	Actual Spending:	$182	$0
	Target Spending:	$1,580	$1,580
	Running % Utilized:	12%	0%

Figure 3.2 Budget expense tracker sample (2/2)

Step 2: Understand basic budgeting principles and rules of thumb.

Here are some general principles and rules of thumb for budgeting. Keep in mind that these are exactly what they say they are: Rules of thumb! If your budget doesn't exactly fit these, don't worry. You may need to adjust if you live in a super high or low cost of living (COL) area.

- 50/30/20 rule: 50% goes to essentials, 30% goes to fun, 20% goes to savings—popularized by U.S. Senator Elizabeth Warren's book *All Your Worth: The Ultimate Lifetime Money Plan*. When you're just starting out, you might not be able to allocate the full 30% to fun, but the savings target of 20% is crucial.
- 15% rule for retirement savings: Save at least 15% of your gross pay to retire by the typical U.S. retirement age (see Section "The 15% Rule for Retirement Calculations" in the appendix for mathematical reasoning). This rule is in line with the above 20% total savings as it should be 15% toward investments and 5% cash for your emergency fund or large purchases.
- 30% rule for housing expense: Spend no more than 30% of your gross pay on your total housing costs, including utilities. This means that your actual housing costs should be more like 25% to leave some room for utilities and repairs, if applicable.

- ○ Note: This is sometimes referred to as the 3× rule for rent, which means that your gross monthly income must be at least 3× the monthly rent, which works out to rent being 33.33% of your gross income.
- 10/50 rule for cars: Spend no more than *10%* of your gross monthly income on your total transportation costs (car payment, maintenance, insurance, gas, etc.). A more general rule is that the purchase price of your vehicle should not exceed *50%* of your annual gross pay.
  - ○ Example: If you make $60k/year, using the 10% rule you should spend no more than $60k/12 × 10% = $500/month on your overall transportation. If using the 50% rule, you should spend no more than $30k purchasing your vehicle (although I recommend that you should be spending way less than 50% of your annual salary on a vehicle).
- 20/3/8 rule for cars: Put *20% down* on your vehicle (including your trade-in if applicable), have a loan for no more than *3 years*, and make sure the total car payment is no more than *8% of your total gross income.*
- 4× rule for homebuying: You should spend no more than 4× your annual gross salary on your home. Banks may approve you for 5 to 6 times your annual salary based upon your debt-to-income ratio (DTI), but it is generally unwise to purchase a house that expensive. Some experts even recommend going down to 3× your salary if you have other outstanding debt or obligations like car loans and student loans.

Step 3: Use rules as guidelines to develop a budget that you are happy with.

Combine your data from Step 1 and the general principles of budgeting from Step 2 to create a budget that fits your lifestyle. See the sample "20XX Budget" tab in the spreadsheet, which takes the U.S. median salary of about $52k/year[7] and breaks it down in a medium cost of living (MCOL) area. Keep in mind that your budget will not be perfect at first. Don't forget to account for taxes by using your take-home pay to calculate how much money you have available to spend each month. If you have been working for a while or have filed taxes before, you should know approximately what percentage of income goes to your taxes by looking at your paycheck or tax filing. If you must guess, you can input your earnings information into an online tax calculator from HR Block, TurboTax, or SmartAsset. They may all give you different answers, so just take the average of the three outcomes. Your budget may be slightly above or below your actual take-home pay, and that is totally fine. In Steps 4 and 5, you will continue to tweak your budget.

Step 4: Continue to track spending.

Tracking your spending is the only way to truly know if you are sticking to your budget. Some people track every penny, some people track every dollar, and some people use apps/services like You Need A Budget (YNAB)[8] to help automate the process. The "20XX Expenses" tab in the spreadsheet is a manual entry system that lets you adjust or categorize everything. Some credit cards track your spending for you, but it is unlikely that you will be able to pay everything with a credit card, so it is still important to track your spending in other accounts to get a holistic view of the money leaving your accounts.

Step 5: Tweak budget as you gain more data.

Use the data that you've gathered to tweak your budget. You shouldn't blindly change your budget to match your spending habits; rather, use your data to identify places to improve or create more space in your budget. For example, you find that you are not going into the office as often as you expect and, therefore, your gas expense is lower than expected. You can now allocate more money to your investments or try new lunch places near your home office. Alternatively, you find that you are not eating out as much and are spending more on groceries to cook at home. You can allocate more of your budget from eating out to spend more on groceries and maybe spend some money getting some new kitchen tools. This will shift your budget toward a more realistic and attainable framework in future years and allow you to set more realistic financial goals. Looking at your list of expenses will also help you understand your spending habits and psychology, which is a bonus.

Sample Budget taken from "20XX Budget" tab. $52k/year net income (about $70k gross), or approximately $1,000/week to spend.

- Essentials   Total: $2,508 per month (59%)
    - Rent + utilities + fees $1,325
    - Car payment + Insurance + Gas $708
    - Health Insurance $150
    - Groceries $325
- Wants/Lifestyle   Total: $746 per month (17%)
    - Food and Drinks $173
    - Travel $300
    - Shopping + Entertainment $273
- Savings (incl. loans)   Total: $1,045 per month (24%)
    - Roth IRA $583
    - Cash Savings $200
    - Student Loans $250
    - Pretax Savings $46

Total: $4,333 per month

Discussion: You may be thinking that this budget is way out of whack with the 50/30/20 rule. It seems imbalanced until you take a closer look at the Student Loans which are listed under savings. From a real-life standpoint, they are essential because you cannot stop paying them without consequences. In terms of budget, the increase to your net worth is equivalent to saving cash (minus the interest paid, which is the cost to borrow). Therefore, they are bucketed under savings and skew the savings rate.

The actual savings rate of this budget, defined by the money that you are keeping to yourself sans the student loans, is 18%. In this instance, it is possible to shift some money from the groceries budget to the food and drinks bucket (cooking vs. eating out). When the emergency fund is built, it would be advantageous to divert that cash flow to Pretax Savings or Roth IRA. Once student loans end, it would be wise to split the cash flow between saving cash for another purchase and improving lifestyle by increasing other areas in the budget.

The other expense that might pop out at you is the transportation cost. The number is much higher than the general recommendation of 10% of gross income ($583/month). The total of $708 per month includes the payment ($250), gas ($108), insurance and registration ($150), and general maintenance ($200). The maintenance inflates the cost of transportation and is generally not included in budgeting guidelines. Note that sans maintenance costs, the monthly cost of transportation is $508, which is less than 10% of gross income. I obviously don't recommend neglecting maintenance on your vehicle, and I only point out that the budgeting rules don't typically consider vehicle maintenance, which is an important aspect of the total cost of vehicle ownership. You can google the average annual maintenance costs for your specific vehicle. Whether you use the entire maintenance allocation is dependent on the condition of your vehicle, but in the best-case scenario you can save this cash toward purchasing a newer vehicle when the time comes.

In a scenario like this, it would be wise for the person in question to attempt to live with a roommate until their car and student loans are paid off. This budget is very tight and does not leave a lot of room for discretionary or emergency spending. The budget is well-balanced, but for financially conscious folks, it might be uncomfortable to live with such small margins. Making the sacrifice of getting a roommate, paying off the car quickly, and paying off student loans will not only free up monthly cash flow for things of greater value but also eliminate the need for a large emergency fund since your baseline monthly expenses will decrease once your loans are paid off—a twofold benefit. Another course of action can be to look at this person's career. Where are they on the income growth curve? If they don't anticipate an increase in income, then they might consider de-risking their financial situation in favor of building a solid financial foundation. If they have high-income potential, they might decide to continue this way knowing that their income will go up shortly. Alternatively, this person could choose to work a second job to supplement their lifestyle expenses such as travel or eating out, so long as they ease off the pedal to prevent burnout after tackling their car and student loans.

Let's take another look at this budget after student and auto loans were paid off and after implementing the aforementioned advice:

- Essentials   Total: $2,258 per month (52%)
  - Rent + utilities + fees $1,325
  - Car maintenance + Insurance + Gas $458
  - Health Insurance $150
  - Groceries $325
- Wants/Lifestyle   Total: $996 per month (23%)
  - Food and Drinks $373
  - Travel $350
  - Shopping + Entertainment $273
- Savings   Total: $1,079 per month (25%)
  - Roth IRA $583
  - Cash Savings $100
  - Pretax Savings $396

Total: $4,333 per month

Discussion: After loans have been paid off, the excess money has been distributed fairly evenly between lifestyle and actual savings. The amount that was being paid toward student loans is now being contributed to a pretax savings account such as a 401(k), 403(b), or IRA. You may be looking at this and thinking that there is literally no space in this budget, and you would be correct. How much wiggle room you provide in your budget is dependent on how closely you track your spending. Ideally, you would want no wiggle room and to know where every cent goes, but, in reality, most people are not going to follow their budget that closely. Planning to utilize 90% to 95% of your available budget is a good rule of thumb. If you do this, theoretically your cash buffer in your checking account will grow over time. If it doesn't, that means you are using more than 100% of your budget.

The balance of a budget will always come down to what kind of lifestyle you want and how much work you are willing to put in, while simultaneously preserving your work–life balance. Aim to focus on the things that bring you value, and once you reach the point where you are getting all the things that bring you value, you can begin to buy your time back in the form of outsourcing your tasks and saving more money for your future, that is, buying back your future time.

Whenever your income rises, it is wise to increase savings by approximately half the amount of the raise. For example, if you are making $70k per year now and saving $15k, and you get a raise to $100k, you should save an additional $15k for a total of $30k per year. Your disposable income has still gone up significantly (over $1,000 per month), and you have increased your savings rate from 21% to 30%. Note that 21% is already a great savings rate, but if you had allocated your entire raise to lifestyle increases, you would only be saving $15k on a $100k salary, which is 15%. Not only has your lifestyle increased, but your savings rate has also decreased—the textbook definition of lifestyle creep. This will make it much harder to save enough for retirement and replace your preretirement lifestyle.

How to Use Your Budget

There are two polar-opposite budget users: people who make their budget and seldom (or never) check it, and people who make their budget and religiously update it after every expense. There are pros and cons to each extreme, but it's up to you to find a balance that works for you. Some people track every penny and some round to the nearest dollar. Most importantly, you must find a combination that you will actually use. A fancy budget is worthless unless you use it. There will also be times in your life when you must stray from your budget: emergencies (you have an emergency fund, right?), unexpected travel, or a super cool once in a lifetime experience. Life isn't about living in a spreadsheet. Some months you might be over on travel and under on gas. Some months you may be over on groceries but under on eating out. As long as you meet your budget approximately each month, you're likely fine over the course of the year. You can use your monthly budget utilization to adjust your spending accordingly. If you go over on "eating out" for a month because you had family visiting, dial it back a bit the next month. If you didn't travel this month, make sure to get out next month and utilize that travel budget!

Lastly, let's touch upon the thought process of making purchases. You may be all excited about this new budget, so excited that you are suddenly afraid to spend money and, thus, go over your budget. There are ways to circumvent this:

- Budget for your next big purchase! A "big purchase" to everyone might vary. It might be $100 or $1,000 or $10,000. The point is, if you want to spend something that might represent a huge chunk of your budget and throw you off, it may be better to have a line in your budget and an associated automatic cash transfer to a savings account.

- Since discovering personal finance, it has been harder for me to spend my hard-earned money. My purchases show up on a spreadsheet after all! However, I have adopted a thought process to help with this. I ask myself, "Is this going to change the bottom line?" Usually, the answer is no. For example, I might be fussing about spending $1,000 on a new TV to replace my tiny 10-year-old TV from college. I will definitely feel a little poorer once I buy it. But if I ask myself if this $1,000 is going to alter the course of my financial journey for the worse? The answer is no. Now if you ask me if it's going to bring me $1,000 worth of utility, only time will tell. Now you might ask, what are some things that DO change the bottom line? Here are a few:
  - Buying a $40k new car (national average right now) results in >$1,000/month for 36 months—that's a new TV every month for 3 years!
  - Unexpectedly having a child or taking on the care of a dependent
  - Getting a luxury apartment for $400 per month more than you're already paying (if you work from home and have no commuting expenses, it might be worth having a nicer apartment. After all, you are spending an additional 160 hours a month inside!)
  - Ordering Doordash twice a day for a total of $60 ($1,800/month)
  - Taking a $10k personal loan at 12% interest and buying a motorcycle or boat that you ride five times a year. Even if you make more than enough to afford a loan like that, double-digit interest rates are always a horrible idea! Generally, toys should be purchased with cash. If you cannot buy a toy with cash, you simply cannot afford it. Put a line item in your budget and contribute to a savings account as if it were a loan payment. If you cannot afford to save cash monthly for a toy, you cannot

afford a monthly loan payment for a toy. Borrowing money for toys is always a bad idea since it gives you the illusion that it's cheaper than it actually is. Once you accumulate the cash for your purchase, you might find that you don't want to spend that lump sum cash on it because you feel that it isn't worth it anymore.

- You know what doesn't change the bottom line? That $5 latte you have every day ($150/month) or a $10 avocado toast once a week ($40/month). Yes, they cost money and yes, they are frivolous purchases (guide on how to make your own coffee at home coming soon). Alas, the number of lattes or avocado toasts that need to be consumed before you surpass one of the big-ticket items listed earlier is bound to make your stomach hurt. Note that the unmonitored accumulation of *things that don't change the bottom line* will eventually change the bottom line, so don't think that just because it's within a certain limit means that you can purchase without thinking.

- For purchases involving monthly payments such as a home or vehicle, utilize the "simulated payment" method where you make the estimated future payment toward a savings account to see if your new cash flow is still feasible. For example, if you are currently paying $1,500 in rent and you want to purchase a home with a mortgage of $2,500, place an additional $1,000 into a savings account to simulate the $2,500 mortgage and see how you do.

- Have a "think before you buy" period. In your mind, there is an amount of money that you would spend without hesitation on something. Anything above that amount requires a minimum 1-week incubation period so you can ask yourself if this item or experience will bring value into your life. For some, it's $50. For some, it's $500. This is not to say that any items below these amounts should be bought without thinking, but that items above that price require a longer period of reflection. You can even have a tiered system; for example, items over $50 require 1 day of incubation; items over $250 require 1 week, and items over $1,000 require 1 month. Many nonessential purchases that we want to make are impulsive purchases. Having this incubation period forces you to sit past the impulsive period. If the desire is still there after the incubation period and it fits in the budget, then more power to you!

- Think about how many hours you need to work to purchase this item or experience. The amount of money that you make per hour amounts to trading time for money, so when you purchase something, you are essentially trading time for that item or experience. This may help or hinder your purchasing psychology, but it is a useful tool in quantifying the value of something to you.

- Consider how much time you would save by purchasing an item. If you're able to spend money to increase your productive hours in your day, you may reap huge benefits down the road. Devoting more attention to your career can yield higher compensation, more time to spend on your relationships, and less stress over the mundane, which will support mental health.

- Consider the dividends that this item or experience will pay you. Oftentimes, we can easily justify purchasing an item because of the time it will save us or the usefulness it might have in our lives. It is much harder to quantify an experience, such as a kayak camping trip down the Nile River, which might be a couple thousand bucks. Although this trip might only last a week, you will remember this trip for your entire life, and every time you think back on this trip and think fondly, you will receive memory dividends. Trips will produce memory dividends forever and cannot be replaced with experiences from other time periods of your life. Even from a material standpoint, it may be beneficial for you to spend $1,000 on a home coffee bar if it will save you $4 per day and a daily trip to the coffee shop. It only takes about 250 coffees to make your money back—less than 1 year of daily coffee!

All in all, find ways to make your budget work for you. You control your budget. Your budget does not control you. Once you get into the rhythm of budgeting and understanding your spending psychology, you will be well on your way to mastering money flow!

Scott's Thoughts: Budgeting Strategy

Over the years, my annual spending has undoubtedly trended upward due to a combination of CPI-based and lifestyle inflation. However, my early-career income growth has far outpaced my spending growth, allowing me to save at a greater rate. At the end of the day, money is a tool for you to be able to live the life you want. As long as you are meeting your savings targets and living within your means, your spending **should** go up year after year. My rule of thumb is that I simply need to save the same or a greater percentage of my income each year than I did the previous year. For example, if my income goes up by $12k/year and I am saving 25% of my income, then my savings should go up by at least $3k/year.

I also accept that I will never have a perfect budget month. Every month there are categories that I spend way too much money on, like a new grill, and categories I spend almost no money on, like car maintenance, if there is no service needed to be addressed. However, I have found that my budget generally evens out at the end of the year as long as I am mindful of my spending. When I started budgeting a few years ago, I looked at my budget before every purchase. Now that I have a feel for my monthly spending, I almost never look at my budget before making a purchase. I have shaped my budget and allocated money toward the lifestyle that I want but have not shifted my lifestyle to make my budgeting spreadsheet look nice. Are there times when I look at something cool and say, "I can't afford that"? Yes! Despite only looking at my budget once or twice a month, my 2023 spending came in at 105% of my budget. Removing a nonessential home renovation put me at 99% budget utilization, which was near perfect.

How Much Rent Can You Afford?

Rent is a much easier calculation because it is a single number! This number should range between 25% and 33% of your total gross pay. Most experts recommend 30% for housing, so 25% + utilities should put you right around the right area. Many landlords require that your monthly gross income must be at least 3× the monthly rent. This percentage of income rule breaks down in two of the following scenarios: very high COL areas such as LA or NYC and for folks with high income (>3× median income).

People who live in very high cost of living (VHCOL) areas sometimes have no choice other than to spend 40% or more of their gross pay going toward housing. However, in these areas it is common not to need a vehicle, which means that one can split their transportation costs between metro and housing. If your salary is not more than 3 times the rent, then you may require a *cosigner* or *guarantor*, which is someone who is on the hook to pay your rent if you are unable to do so. You can (should) also get a roommate to split the cost.

People who make much higher than the median income may deviate from this rule due to diminishing returns after a certain level of housing and the fact that their income is taxed at a higher rate and will therefore result in lower net pay. It is best to use your judgment and only get what you can comfortably afford and will reasonably use. In general, the best way to circumvent high rent is to get a roommate. It is a sacrifice, but it is oftentimes better than living in a lower quality and sometimes more dangerous apartment or area. Being closer to work is also advantageous because it saves time and money in the commuting space. Only you can decide whether you prefer to supplement the cost of housing via a roommate or moving to a cheaper area.

Buying Versus Renting Home

There is a consensus in our culture that buying a home is better than renting. Here, we will look at both sides of the story and show that it isn't as clear-cut as one might think. The key difference between buying and renting is NOT that buying builds equity. The real difference is the risk profile—a huge factor that most people don't consider.

Pros of purchasing: You can build equity via mortgage payoff while potentially experiencing home value appreciation.[9] You are also able to make the home more suited for your lifestyle by modifying it. The principal and interest payment is fixed for the life of the loan, granted you have a conventional mortgage and not an adjustable rate mortgage (ARM). In certain areas such as California, there are laws in place that govern the maximum increase to property tax in any given year, which work in favor of the homeowner. Lastly, mortgages tend to be cheaper or comparable to rents for similar-style homes *in the long run.*

Cons of purchasing: Your mortgage is the lowest amount you'll pay each month, guaranteed. If you purchase a home that is relatively old, you will need to factor the cost of repairs into your purchase price. Be prepared for sticker shock when you find out how much it costs to re-place a roof or do a simple repainting. You are locked into around 5 years to break even on your transactional costs of homeownership via equity building. Lastly, while the equity in your home is a positive contribution to your net worth as is any principal paid into your mortgage, the equity is not liquid at all, meaning you cannot access that cash easily. You would have to do potentially complex things to access that equity, which, in turn, costs money.

It is important always to check the cost of buying versus renting com-parable properties. Many people make the mistake of comparing the cost of renting a townhome versus purchasing an apartment, or vice versa. Make sure to compare apples to apples, since it is easy to cherry-pick numbers to satisfy your confirmation bias.

The bottom line is that unless you have very specific needs that can only be met by purchasing a home *and* you know that you will be stay-ing in a particular area for a few years *and* you have enough cash in your reserves to handle any surprise projects that might come up, then renting is actually not a bad choice financially! Ultimately, it's a matter of what is best for you and your lifestyle and financial goals.

Scott's Thoughts: Housing Philosophy

I will get this one out of the way early: Renting is not throwing away money. Many people believe that renting is a waste. When you rent, you're not only paying for housing and a small premium for flexibility but also paying for the security of not having to maintain anything. Another huge misconception about buying versus renting is that peo-ple assume that your mortgage is a fixed cost. While your principal and interest might not change throughout the life of the loan, your insurance, maintenance, and property tax are almost guaranteed to go up. Home maintenance costs only go up as your home gets older. There are very specific requirements that have to be met until you can firmly say that homeownership is right for you from a financial standpoint. Most people are better off renting until they absolutely know what they want in life. Many people falsely believe that building equity in a home is a requirement in order to build wealth. While building equity in a home is a nice bonus, it is the icing on top of the cake and should not be the main reason for purchasing a home. You should have a very specific need or goal in mind when purchasing a home apart from building equity. Remember that having equity in a primary residence doesn't do anything for you unless the house is paid off or you're rolling your equity into another home, which involves transactional costs. It is much more financially prudent to prioritize funding your retirement investments than trying to stretch to pay for a house.

The cost of purchasing a home is astronomically high. You pay 2% to 3% of the purchase price in closing costs in addition to the down payment. If you were to sell that home, you would have to pay some percentage (usually 6%) of the sale price in realtor fees.

Everyone who owns a home has to have an exit strategy, and they must understand their breakeven timeline. When I purchased my home, I knew that I had to stay in it for 5 years in order for it to be worth the transactional fees. Additionally, I plan to rent out the home if I move somewhere else and selling is not an option. I was mentally prepared to be a landlord—not everybody is.

Nonetheless, if you know you will stay in the same area for at least a few years, can afford to purchase a home, and are prepared to spend money on unexpected repairs, then by all means! As long as you are prepared and have realistic expectations, then you are on the right path. There are amazing benefits to purchasing a home as long as you understand the pros and cons. Keep in mind that as your mortgage rises, your income will theoretically rise as well. Your income should outpace your mortgage growth, so your mortgage should become a smaller and smaller portion of your paycheck.

How Much Car Can You Afford?

The recommended cost for a car was discussed earlier in this chapter. However, it is important to note that just because it falls into your budget, doesn't necessarily mean that you should spend that money on a vehicle. Purchasing an expensive new vehicle is one of the most financially debilitating choices a young professional can make, and it only results in a marginal quality of life improvement. You may have heard your old-school parents say, "You should buy a brand-new vehicle so you don't have to worry about maintenance" or "You should buy a luxury vehicle so that you can impress your coworkers and climb the corporate ladder." If you've gotten this far in this book, your bogus alarm should already be going off. The best vehicle you can own is a paid-off vehicle—end of story. As long as the vehicle you have is safe, reasonably reliable, and fits your lifestyle, it is likely the best vehicle for you.

A caveat to not purchasing a nicer car than what your needs require is if cars are your hobby. You may be able to justify spending more than what's recommended on a vehicle if it's genuinely your hobby! As with all things finance, you need to be able to prioritize where your money is going. You may love cars but hardly eat out or travel (or vice versa). You may be able to allocate some of your eating out allowance toward transportation. The way to hash this out on a budget is as follows:

- You allocate the "essential" portion of your budget to go toward buying the reasonable bare minimum vehicle that will get you from Point A to Point B safely and reliably.
- Anything above that is seen as a "discretionary" expense and is technically considered a want, not a need.

The bottom line is that there is a minimum reasonable amount of money you need to spend on reliable transportation. Anything more than the "bare minimum" is a luxury and should be considered as such. This concept of essential versus luxury can be applied to anything in your budget, for example, groceries are considered essential while eating out is considered a luxury even though both are food.

The monthly cost of your car depends on the loan amount, interest rate, and loan term. Dealership salesmen will attempt to get you fixated on a monthly payment and stretch the loan terms to match your payment desires, even if the car is out of your budget. To avoid this fallacy, you must focus on the total purchase price of the vehicle and not the monthly payment. Follow the 10/50 rule or 20/3/8 rule for car purchases as guidelines.

Let's discuss the other costs of car ownership: insurance and maintenance. Unlike the purchase price and financing costs of a car, these can vary widely. Your insurance depends on a plethora of factors such as your age, location, driving history, the type of vehicle you drive, and so on. You should always shop around for insurance quotes *before* you purchase a new vehicle. Many people go from driving econoboxes to similarly priced sports cars and are shocked that their insurance doubles or triples. Additionally, the maintenance costs of your vehicle can be unpredictable. This unpredictability is one of the reasons people choose to buy new cars. However, the incremental cost of a new car will almost always exceed the maintenance costs of a slightly used car, especially a used one that is still under warranty. New cars also depreciate way faster than used cars.

In terms of maintenance, there are normal wear and tear items and major repairs. Normal wear and tear items you should budget for include oil changes, tires, brakes, air filters, and so on. Major repairs might come out of your emergency fund and are things such as engine problems, transmission repair, drivetrain wear, and so on. If you have an older car, I recommend contributing additional money toward your maintenance fund. If you drive a luxury vehicle, both parts and labor are going to be more expensive, oftentimes exceeding double that of an economy vehicle. If you buy an older luxury vehicle for $30k that once retailed for $100k, you are still maintaining a $100k vehicle. It isn't intrinsically wrong to buy an older vehicle; you just need to factor a slightly higher cost of maintenance into your budget or learn how to maintain it yourself! On a side note, learning how to perform basic maintenance on your vehicle will save you a ton of money in the long run. For reference, "shop time" for repair shops is usually between $150/hour and $300/hour depending on the type of shop (dealer vs. independent) or specialty (Japanese vs. European). Changing your cabin air filter yourself takes less than 5 minutes and costs around $10 for the part, but shops charge $50 to do it since they'll charge 15 minutes of labor. You can decide if that's worth it to you.

The formula to calculate your total cost of ownership (TCO) of your vehicle over a certain period of ownership is:

$$[\text{TCO}] = [\text{Purchase price}] + [\text{Tax and fees}] + [\text{Fuel cost}]$$
$$+ [\text{Insurance premium}] + [\text{Maintenance cost}] - [\text{Blue book value}]$$

One of the biggest expenses you'll incur in car ownership is actually depreciation, which is: [purchase price] − [blue book value]. Contrary to logic, cars that cost less but depreciate more can have higher TCO than cars that cost more but depreciate less. You can find the average annual depreciation for any vehicle that you're interested in by searching it up online or calculate it by searching up used specimens and using the following formula:

$$\left[\text{Depreciation rate}\right] = 1 - \left(\frac{\left[\text{Current price}\right]}{\left[\text{MSRP}\right]}\right)^{\frac{1}{\left[\text{Current year}\right] - \left[\text{Car model year}\right]}}$$

A common fallacy people succumb to is that they need to buy a new vehicle when the cost of repairing or fixing their vehicle exceeds the vehicle's value. All other things equal, it only makes mathematical sense if the cost to repair your current vehicle exceeds the cost of purchasing a new vehicle. Consider the following scenario:

You have a used sedan that was worth around $5,000 before the transmission broke. The transmission needs to be replaced along with some other routine repairs like brakes, tires, and so on. Your mechanic quotes you $6,000 to perform the required services. You think, "This is going to cost more than the value of my car," so you sell this car for $3,000 (a discount due to the problems) and then you finance a $15,000 used car that might give you a host of other problems since you know nothing about this car. For simplicity, let's ignore any potential new problems. Your total cost here is $15,000 plus the $2,000 loss you took on selling your old car. Not only have you sold your current car for a loss, but you have also taken on new debt by purchasing another vehicle. You *may* be better off fixing your current car for $6,000 and continue to drive it while you save up for another car. The total cost here is just $6,000, which is $9,000 cheaper than purchasing a newer car. The glaring difference between the two scenarios here is that in Scenario 1 you have a new (used) car whereas in Scenario 2 you have the same car as before. While that is certainly a notable difference, oftentimes people are forced to rush these decisions since not having transportation can be a big problem. Additionally, notice that the $6,000 repair quote includes routine maintenance as well, which every car needs. The non-routine emergency repair might only be a fraction of the total cost. In the midst of making a quick decision, you may make emotional or irrational decisions that you may regret in the future. This is another reason why understanding your psychological relationship with money is so important.

Clearly, I have crafted a very specific scenario that may very well not pertain to your personal situation. However, the point is to drive home that the tipping point of purchasing a new vehicle is not necessarily when the cost of repairs exceeds the value of the vehicle.

Note: When purchasing a used car, always get a Pre-Purchase Inspection (PPI) from a reputable third-party mechanic. They cost a couple hundred dollars and can save you a ton of headache down the road.

Should You Purchase a More Fuel-Efficient Vehicle?

You may consider purchasing a more fuel-efficient vehicle to replace your current vehicle. The payback of having a fuel-efficient vehicle is not as much as you think unless you drive an astronomical amount. As usual, it comes down to a math exercise—let's look at an example.

Assumptions:

- It's 2023 and you drive 50 miles each day to go to and from work, 5 days per week, and on the weekends you drive approximately 100 miles. Your total mileage is 350 miles per week.

- You drive a 2014 Toyota Highlander V6, which gets 20 MPG combined.
- Your Highlander currently has a book value of $18,000.
- Gas is $3.00/gallon.
- Assume insurance and maintenance remain the same for the new and old vehicle (it's a Toyota!)
- Depreciation is not considered

Currently, you burn 17.5 gallons of fuel per week, which comes out to $52.50/week of fuel. You are considering purchasing a 2023 Toyota Rav4 Hybrid to replace this vehicle. The Rav4 gets an astonishing 40 MPG and costs between $30,000 and $40,000. Let's assume a mid-trim model which runs $35,000. Trading in your Highlander for the Rav4 will cost $17,000, not including transaction fees like sales tax, registration, and so on. Your weekly cost of fuel for your Rav4 is $26.25, resulting in a difference of $26.25. This will take 648 weeks to recuperate, or approximately 12.5 years! Even if you were to drive double the distance weekly (over 700 miles per week), it would still take over 6 years to recuperate the cost. Not to mention that new vehicles depreciate more quickly than used vehicles! The bottom line is that as long as your vehicle is reliable, it rarely makes sense to trade it for a more fuel-efficient car if it will cost you significantly more money. Mathematically, fuel consumption (and therefore cost) is inversely related to your fuel economy.

$$\text{fuel cost} = \text{miles driven} / \text{fuel economy}$$

This means that it's nonlinear. Going from 10 MPG to 20 MPG will decrease your fuel cost by half, or 50%, but going from 20 MPG to 30 MPG only decreases your fuel cost by 33%. Going from 30 MPG to 40 MPG decreases your fuel cost by only 25%. In order to continue halving your fuel costs, your fuel economy needs to double.

However, if you are in the market for a new vehicle due to lifestyle changes or reliability issues, then it is certainly worth looking at more fuel-efficient models to help keep fuel costs as low as possible if that's important to you!

How to Manage Cash Windfall

Not knowing what to do with an unexpected influx of cash is not the worst problem to have! It is imperative to know what to do when provided with any chunk of money outside of your normal income. Such surprises can come from bonuses (which you should generally not include in your budgeting calculation), inheritances, lottery/casino winnings, sale of property, insurance payouts, and so on. In general, the best way to handle windfall cash is to follow the personal finance flowchart. First and foremost, set aside the appropriate amount for taxes, if applicable. Second, fully fund your emergency fund. Third, pay off high-interest debt (>5%). Fourth, max out tax-advantaged retirement account space for the year and set aside money for your IRA for the next year. Fifth, take 5% to 10% of the money and go on vacation or buy something nice for yourself (or do that first—it's your money). Sixth, save for large purchases like a home or car in a high-yield savings account (HYSA). Lastly, invest the rest in a taxable account (more on that later).

How Much Is Enough to Save?

The amount of income required for a single person with no dependents to save aggressively is not as high as you might think. There are huge misconceptions that you need a minimum income or minimum amount of money to begin saving and investing. That is a lie that many people tell themselves to avoid having to buckle down and start saving. As long as you have the ability to earn enough income to cover your expenses, you have enough to save even just a few dollars every month. At some point, your ability to save money is dependent on your ability to hustle. Once you make enough money to cover your barebone expenses, you can dedicate the rest of your cash flow to building a solid financial foundation. You must build a financial foundation so as not to fall into the dangerous trap of borrowing money to stay afloat. If you believe that you aren't able to save any money, then you should just save $1 a month. You then might increase that to $1 a week. Then perhaps you might increase it to $1 per day. The logic behind this is that not only are you slowly and quantitatively moving toward a better financial future, but you are also building the habits that will help you save more money in the future when your income is higher!

Net Worth and Savings Targets

You may wonder how you're doing financially compared with everyone else. The most popular way to compare your financial health with that of everyone else is to compare salaries or savings/investments. However, those are far from the best methods since people have vastly different life-styles. The main component in determining your "place" in the rat race is your net worth as a multiple of your income, as a function of your age (from the book *The Millionaire Next Door*).

Your net worth is a dollar amount that shows your total assets minus liabilities. This number can help indicate whether you're on the right path or not. In general, you want your net worth to rise every month. Note that this doesn't necessarily mean that your assets rise each month. An equivalent decrease in debt has a similar effect on net worth: [Net Worth] = [Assets] - [Debts]. If you find your net worth decreasing each month, you are essentially digging yourself into a hole that will become increasingly difficult to get out of. From a mathematical standpoint, reducing your assets is just as detrimental as increasing debt. Note that swings in the market value of your assets can cause your net worth to decrease in the short term, especially when you have a large amount tied to market investments. Therefore, it's important to understand the source of changes in your net worth. Let's discuss the aforementioned methods and some target benchmarks:

$$[\text{Expected Net Worth}] = [\text{Age}] \times [\text{Gross Annual Income}]/10$$
$$- [\text{Inherited Wealth}]$$

In other words, for every 10 years of age, you should have approximately $1\times$ your annual salary saved up (minus any inherited wealth, since inherited wealth doesn't reflect your ability to save money and build wealth):

- 30 years old: $3\times$ salary in net worth
- 40 years old: $4\times$ salary in net worth
- 50 years old: $5\times$ salary in net worth

Of course, the younger you are, the less realistic this formula is. Most people begin working between ages 21 and 23. Having 3× your annual salary saved in 7 to 9 years while trying to pay off student loans is simply unrealistic. The more realistic expectation is to have

- 30 years old: 1× salary in net worth
- 40 years old: 4× salary in net worth
- 50 years old: 10× salary in net worth
- 60 years old: 20× salary in net worth

While this configuration may seem even more ludicrous, you will find that compound interest makes it much easier to save later in life because the money you have already saved is working hard for you. The reality is that you will experience exponential growth, rather than linear growth with the previous benchmark. Note that this guidance does not differ whether you're married or single or have kids. They also don't take into account how much of your salary you save. They are simply litmus tests to see whether or not you are on approximately the right path. Whichever philosophy you choose, working toward these targets will give you peace of mind as you progress through life! (Figure 3.3).

Produced by saving 12% of your salary and a growth rate of 7%. In this scenario, you are plenty shy of 3× salary by 30 years old, but you

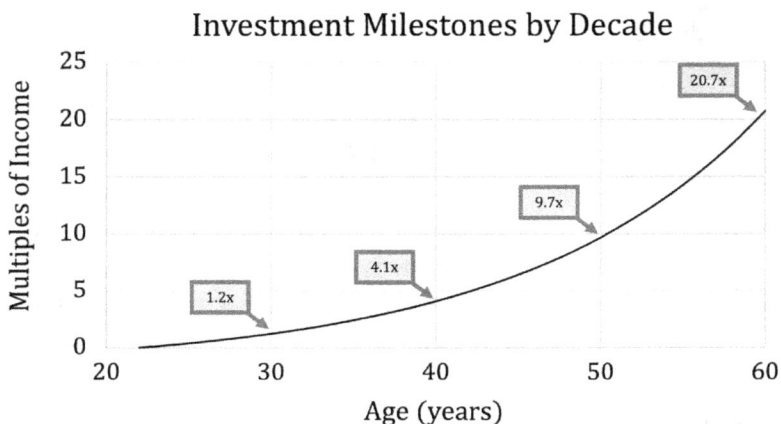

Figure 3.3 Investment milestones by decade

have handily exceeded the 4× and 5× salary savings targets by the time you are 40 and 50 years old, respectively. Continuing this for another 10 to 15 years will get you to the 20 to 25× range, the perfect amount for a comfortable retirement. Compound growth is so beautiful!

There are some other financial targets you may consider trying to achieve before a certain age, some quantifiable and some psychological. The age of intent for these goals is 40. If you hit even a handful of them, you are in great shape! Some of these goals are simply mentality shifts that can occur at any time. However, to internalize them completely takes years. In no particular order, here we go:

- 6+ month emergency fund in a HYSA. You should steadily increase the number until retirement. Many personal finance pros say that you should have at least one and even up to three years of liquid cash in retirement.
- Understanding the *anything versus everything mentality*—you can have anything you want but not everything you want.
- Implement the 5/25 rule[10] made famous by Warren Buffet. You make a list of your top 5 priorities (A list) and 25 other priorities (B list) underneath that. You only focus on the top 5 priorities and actively NOT focus on the other 25. This will help you focus on the biggest priorities in your life. Once you achieve your top 5 goals, you remake the list, potentially moving items from the B list to the A list.
- Another Warren Buffet quote: "If you were given a punch card with 20 punches on it and for each financial decision you made in your life you made a punch, you'd get very rich. Because you'd think very hard about each decision."
- Zero debt except mortgage.
- 800+ credit score.
- 5× your annual spending in investments. Essentially, this is a very rough number for CoastFIRE. For example, if your annual spending is $80k and you have $400k, you can stop contributing to retirement, and, in 20 years at 8% return, you'd be able to withdraw 4% of your $1.86M balance that gives around $74k/ year. Again, a *very* rough CoastFIRE benchmark but an important one nonetheless.

- Make a will or set up a trust depending on your net worth.
- Have the appropriate term life insurance policy set up if you have people who depend on your income.
- Be healthy! Your decision to pay attention to your health is one of the biggest financial decisions you could ever make. Healthcare cost inflation has been historically higher than standard inflation.
- Figure out the bucket list items that you won't be able to do once you get older; this is not a financial tip, but many people focus so much on saving to retire that they don't spend their youthful years doing things only their young self can do.

CHAPTER 4

Financial Organization

Before we proceed, it is imperative to talk about how to keep your finances organized. In this section, we will discuss the tools and structure you can use to keep yourself organized and make your life easy. An organized financial portfolio is the foundation of an efficient portfolio. Let's discuss the accounts and tools first and then we will discuss putting the pieces together. Keep in mind that it isn't critical to use all these tools or methods, but rather to be aware of them in case your personal financial management philosophy requires such tools.

Accounts and Tools

- Checking Account: The most frequently used account that you will have. This is the account that your paycheck will route to and the account from which you will pay all of your bills. Since this account is high traffic, you are at higher risk of fraud or theft. Therefore, it is best to keep just enough to float about 2 to 4 weeks or 1 to 2 paychecks worth of cash in the account in the event that some unexpected interruption happens in your cash flow. If you are financially organized, you really shouldn't be getting frequent unexpected withdrawals or overdrafts.
- Savings Account: This is a standard savings account that is attached directly to your checking account under the same bank. That way, you can instantly transfer money to your checking account in the event that you need it. The savings account should contain about 1 month of expenses and no more. The exception to this rule is if you are saving up for a large purchase in the near future and don't want to use your primary checking account.
- HYSA: This account has a higher interest rate than a standard savings account, so it is advantageous to keep as much of your liquid cash

in there as possible. In general, it's best to keep most of emergency expense cash in your HYSA. This is also the place where you might keep cash savings for a home down payment or a vacation fund. You can have more than one HYSA under your name, so separate funds as necessary. Some banks allow you to make buckets under the same account to help you separate your savings. Be aware of the FDIC-insured limit of $250k. You are welcome to keep as much as you'd like in your account, but only the first $250k of each account will be insured by the government in case something happens to your bank.

- Daily-Use Credit Card: There are a ton of options, so be sure to research a card that meets your daily needs. There is a common misconception that credit cards with annual fees are automatically bad. If the benefits of the card outweigh the annual fee, it may be worth your consideration.

- Backup Credit Card: This is your card that you can rely on in case your primary card is declined, stolen, or inaccessible. Years ago, American Express and Discover were not accepted in certain establishments. Although it is better now, there are still establishments that do not take all forms of credit cards. Therefore, it is a good idea to carry more than one card that is different from your primary card. There is also a misconception that having multiple credit cards is bad for your credit. That is false. Abusing your credit cards by spending more than you can afford on multiple credit cards is bad for your credit and financial health. Simply having multiple lines of credit is not detrimental to your credit. In fact, having credit diversity and high credit limits can positively impact your credit score—more on that in the next chapter.

- Taxable Brokerage Account: This is where you will do some of your non–tax-advantaged investing. This is a vehicle that carries your investments and acts as a portal that allows you to buy and sell your stock investments. Don't worry about what that means now, just know that you need one of these accounts.

- Roth/Pretax IRA: These accounts are tax-advantaged accounts that have low annual contribution limits but are powerful tools in your portfolio. Your choice of Roth versus Pretax will depend on your tax diversification strategy and eligibility.

- 401(k)/403(b)/Equivalent: This account is typically sponsored via your employer (or yourself via solo-401(k) if you are your own employer). This account is funded via automatic deductions from your paycheck. Always check with your company and financial provider for the specifics of your account.

- Net Worth Tracker: This is not an account but a tool that tracks your financial health. Recall that your net worth is your assets minus your debts. Keeping track of this on a regular basis is crucial to understanding your financial position. Some folks update this monthly, while others do it quarterly or annually. Whichever frequency you choose is completely up to you. It may be demoralizing to see a low or even negative net worth when you are just starting out, but you will feel a great sense of empowerment and encouragement when you see the amount grow each month from your hard work. As long as you are making money and spending within your means, your net worth should increase over time! Having a tracker will help you visualize that growth and encourage you to continue chugging along.

Beware: Identity Theft

Identify theft affects approximately 1 million[11] people each year. Due to the vast availability of information and inevitable digital footprint left behind by everything you do, it is nearly impossible to eliminate the risk of identity theft. Nonetheless, you can take the following steps to reduce your risk:

1. Minimize your digital footprint online by removing unnecessary information. You can do this yourself or pay a service to do it for you.
2. Lock your credit report down at the three credit bureaus.
3. Create strong passwords and don't reuse passwords for different accounts.
4. Only carry the documentation and cards that you need and use regularly.
5. Shred unnecessary documents that contain sensitive information.
6. Review your financial accounts regularly and check for unexpected activity.

- Expense Tracker: In addition to what has already been discussed in the budgeting section, it is advantageous to note monthly or annual expenses to know when they are expected to be withdrawn from your account. For example, I am always surprised by my annual Amazon Prime subscription or my biannual car insurance payment, but if I have it written in my expense tracker (and/or calendar), I will know that it's coming up.

Where to Park Your Cash

The most common place to park cash is in a HYSA. These accounts are generally provided by banks that do not have physical locations and operate only virtually. However, they offer a great place to store your money due to the relatively high interest rate versus a regular checking or savings account. The money is also fairly liquid and can be accessed within a few days. Your choice of HYSA is not important as long as it is FDIC-insured and has low or no fees or minimum balances.[12] Popular banks, in no particular order, include:

- Sofi
- American Express
- Discover
- Ally
- Marcus (by Goldman Sachs)
- Synchrony

Another place to park your cash is bonds. Whereas banks typically loan money out to consumers in exchange for interest and principal paid in return, bonds are loans from consumers to businesses that will be paid back to consumers via interest and principal. In a similar vein, Certificate of Deposits (CDs) are set amounts of money you loan to a bank for a set amount of time and set interest rate. These can be great if you know that you are not going to access your money for a minimum amount of time.

Most cash that you keep liquid is for an emergency fund. While you may not need all of it at once, you may need some of it. While you can place some of your holdings in bonds or CDs, there is a technique that you can use to maintain a moderate amount of liquidity while taking advantage of the higher rate of return from bonds and CDs versus a HYSA: A bond or CD ladder.

Suppose you want to balance returns and liquidity for an $18,000 emergency fund. Your HYSA is paying 3.5% interest, but CDs are paying 4.5% interest. You place $9,000 into your HYSA earning 3.5%. You take the remaining $9,000 and every month for 6 months, you use $1,500 of it and purchase 6-month CDs. By the time you have purchased your 6th CD, your first CD has reached maturity, and you have the option to either purchase another one or roll that money back into your HYSA.

You are able to perform a ladder with practically any amount in any duration. For example, I could have made two purchases of $4,500 for 1-year CDs in 6-month increments, which would give me a maturing CD every 6 months versus 1 month. This strategy allows you to claim that extra 1% interest rate and have a moderate amount of liquidity. As mentioned, there are few things in life that will use up your entire emergency fund, so it might make sense to allocate a portion of it to a less liquid asset to generate slightly higher returns. Whether it's worth the extra work is up to you. Note that interest rates will change as you roll through your ladder just as they will in your HYSA.

Whether the additional work is worth the extra 1% is up to you!

On the flip side, if you are saving for a down payment for a home, and you know for sure that you are not going to shop for some time, it may be wise to purchase a CD so you can lock in a slightly higher return. All in all, the three tools (HYSA, bonds, CDs) that you can use to park money involve different rates of return, flexibility, and liquidity. Together you can use them to achieve your desired level of liquidity and return!

Putting It All Together

Simply having the aforementioned accounts is not enough to guarantee financial organization. Your first order of business is to use each account as intended. To facilitate this, you should utilize automation wherever and whenever possible. For most folks, automating payments to credit cards, money transfers to investment accounts and savings, and expense tracking will reduce your monthly workload a ton. Automation will help you stay on top of your personal finance game without relying on your discipline. Everyone's discipline is limited, and discipline fatigue is a real thing; it's part of human nature. Having the proper systems in place will allow you to meet your goals without having to think about them constantly. This will allow you to use your discipline in other areas of your life! Here are some things you can automate to improve your monthly financial workflow and organization:

- Credit card payments
    - Be sure to pay off your statement balance each month, not just the minimum payment.
- Transfers from checking account to savings accounts
- Transfers from checking account to investment accounts
- Actions in your investment accounts (investing in your fund of choice on a regular basis)
- Bill payments
    - Be sure to set calendar alerts or e-mails for variable bills so you're not blindsided by a $1,000 water bill that causes you to overdraft.

As you continue on your personal finance journey, you will have a better idea of how much money you need in each of your checking/savings accounts and can adjust accordingly. You might also consider changing the due dates of your credit cards and bills so that everything comes at once (perhaps on the day you get paid). As long as your method works for you, it is a win! When you first start out, it is a good idea to mark the important transfer dates on your calendar, so you know when they are coming up. There is a possibility that the transfer might not go through if it was set up incorrectly, or there may be insufficient funds to make the transfer, or the transfer might take longer than expected. Whatever the reason, keeping an eye on things the first few months is crucial to making sure all continues to go smoothly when you are no longer watching.

Financial Organization with Your Significant Other

Your choice of life partner will be the single largest financial decision you make in your life. I repeat: Your choice of life partner will be the single largest financial decision you make in your entire life. This is not at all saying to marry rich; rather, make sure your significant other has similar financial philosophy and goals. On the other hand, think twice about marrying someone who has a lot of unsecured debt. When you combine finances in marriage, debt becomes shared. A 2017 study with over 1,000 participants done by Ramsay Solutions showed that almost half of couples with more than $50k in consumer debt say that money is a top reason for arguments. Your money management philosophy is closely tied to lifestyle preferences. One person wants a big house but a cheap car, and the other person wants a small house but three nice cars. One person wants to eat out every day while the other person wants to cook at home and spend that money on travel. One person might want to save a lot to retire early and live modestly while the other person might want to work forever and not save to live a fancy lifestyle. Keep in mind that, short of having an obscene amount of money, you simply cannot afford everything that you want and so compromise must occur. In whatever form the disagreements come, you should iron those things out long before marriage is even considered. Your spouse can be the ultimate wealth-building tool if you are both on the same page about spending and lifestyle and also help build each other up by supporting your careers and life goals. By contrast, disagreements and divorces are extremely costly and stressful.

In terms of splitting things financially, there isn't one right way to go about this. You will meet many couples who do things differently. Here are some of the most common ways to organize your finances with a significant other:

- If both spouses work, then you may find a 50/50 split to be perfect. For couples with similar income levels, this may be ideal so that both partners are equal stakeholders in the relationship.
- If one person makes significantly more money than the other person, then splitting based on income may be appropriate. For example, if one person makes $100k and the other makes $50k, one person makes two-thirds of the total household income (HHI), and the other person makes one-third of the HHI. If rent is $2,400, then in this scenario the person making $100k would contribute $1,600 to the rent and the person making $50k would

contribute $800. That way, the contribution for each person is the same portion of their individual income, and they share the same relative financial burden.

- Some modification of the percentage method, which still involves the person making more money contributing more but perhaps not to the extreme described earlier.

- If one person doesn't work at all, then of course it would be 100/0. There isn't anything intrinsically wrong with this—this is how it was frequently done for decades until the COL rose significantly in recent years.

Of course, these are guidelines. You may be saying, "If I truly love my significant other, I won't mind paying for everything and I won't want my significant other to work!" That may be 100% true and very noble of you. However, many individuals want to contribute for their own reasons/ sense of purpose or build a fulfilling career. As long as you have a proper adult conversation with your significant other about finances and both are able to stick to a plan, then the risk of things going awry will be greatly reduced.

From an accounting perspective, there is a multitude of ways to manage finances. One of the most sensible is to have a shared account that each person contributes a designated amount to each month that will go toward shared expenses such as savings, rent/mortgage, utilities, groceries, and so on. The rest of your money can go into personal accounts that can be used for whatever you each want. This eliminates the "Can I buy this?" questions from your spouse. The money that is your own after contributing your portion to household expenses is strictly "free-use" money and can be used as such. Of course, you may still find yourself buying things or experiences for your partner or vice versa (such as a nice dinner out). How much you contribute to each account will be completely up to you and your partner. In addition to a common shared checking account, you may also have a combined savings account to save for big purchases such as a vacation, a new home, or home renovations. All investment accounts must remain separate, but you can list each other as beneficiaries in the event of death.

Another way to manage finances is simply to merge everything together and go from there. Many couples do this and it is not an intrinsically bad way to go about organizing joint finances, especially if you and your spouse are on the same page financially. However, it can lead to issues down the road due to lack of clarity on who is spending money on what. Through many discussions with young couples throughout the years, I have found that when accounts are merged, one person in the relationship knows far more about money and their financial situation than the other person. It ends up being one person who manages the money. Not only does this lay the grounds for subtle financial manipulation, but it also does the less educated person no good in the event of divorce. Not all couples fight about money, but many couples do. Keeping your organization skills up to date and having mature conversations with your significant other will help reduce the odds of fighting about money.

Note that the methods discussed in this section are for married couples. It is ill-advised to combine finances with someone with whom you are not married. This is due to the legal and financial complications if you should separate. For the same reason, it is not advised to purchase a home with your significant other if you are not married. Speaking of separation, a prenuptial agreement is something you should at least consider. A prenup is sort of like insurance for a marriage in the event of separation. It lets everyone determine who gets to take each part of what was accumulated during the marriage. "I am not going to get a divorce!" Statistically, you have a relatively high likelihood of getting one (nearly 50% of all married couples in the United States do). Not planning for failure is planning to fail. Nobody gets in the car and puts on their seatbelt with the intention of ever needing it. Besides, the best time to determine the asset split is when you are in a good place in your relationship.

Does Getting Married Actually Save You Money?

You might hear a lot of advice from people telling you that getting married will help you move more quickly toward your financial goals. While that may be true in certain situations, it's not a surefire way to improve your financial health. The reason that this myth exists is because of taxes. The only time when you gain a tax advantage as a married couple is when one partner makes significantly more than the other partner. The person making more money pays more in taxes, and then after marriage, the money made in the highest tax bracket gets transferred to the lower tax bracket of the lesser-earning partner. Consider the extremely simplified example:

- Sally makes $200k per year and is in the 32% federal tax bracket as a single filer.
- Sam makes $40k per year and is in the 12% federal tax bracket as a single filer.

Note that this does not mean that they pay 32% and 12% of their total income toward taxes (more on this later); it simply means that the next dollar that they earn will be taxed at 32% and 12%, respectively. Their HHI is $240k per year and, therefore, if they file as married, their marginal tax bracket is 24%. Essentially, the money that Sally makes will get transferred to Sam as income and will go toward the 12% bracket so that the 32% bracket is not touched at all.

This method does not work if both spouses make the same amount of money. When both spouses make the same amount of money, the brackets essentially double and the income in each tax bracket will double.

There are other financial benefits to getting married, such as sharing health or military benefits, splitting housing and utilities, and even sharing vehicles if living in the same household. Despite all this, you should not get married solely for financial security. That is a recipe for disaster!

Insurance

Insurance is something that almost everyone has and yet is commonly misunderstood. It is used to trade small guaranteed losses in exchange for a large unlikely loss. The small guaranteed loss is your premium while the large unlikely loss is your coverage. In car insurance, it's an accident or theft; in health insurance, it's an unexpected visit to the emergency room; in flood insurance, it's, well, a flood. Insurance companies accept your continuous monthly payment for partial or complete coverage of large losses. When a large loss occurs, they protect you by paying out the damages. All of this might not be news to you, but let's discuss the fundamental mathematics behind insurance and how it might impact your decision when choosing insurance that is right for you.

In order for an insurance company to make money, they must pull in at least as much premiums as they pay out in claims and spend on operations. Therefore, an insurance company runs analyses on each of their customers to determine their likelihood of filing a claim. For example, a car insurance company might look at your driving history, demographics, type of vehicle you're driving, and location to determine your overall risk as a driver, while a flood insurance company might look at the historical likelihood of flooding in your area along with the type of drainage you have in your home. Insurance does not work with a small group of people or on an individual basis—if it did, you would simply pay your premiums into your own piggy bank and withdraw it when you need to make a claim. In order for insurance to work, it must be aggregated to all of the customers of that insurance network.

Generally speaking, there are two primary aspects in your insurance strategy that you need to consider for choosing insurance: Your desired coverage and your risk profile. In some types of insurance, your coverage will be based on what you are insuring. More expensive cars and homes are more expensive to insure. You are also able to add additional coverage, such as uninsured motorist coverage, or sewer coverage for your home. For a certain amount of coverage, the insurance plan that you choose will come down to your risk tolerance. A person with a higher risk tolerance will choose a plan with a lower monthly premium in exchange for a higher deductible in the event of a claim. A person with a lower risk tolerance will choose a plan with a higher monthly premium but a lower deductible.

Some folks will say that high deductibles are automatically bad, which is not necessarily true. As usual, it comes down to a math exercise, which the insurance company has already done before even offering you coverage. You can easily calculate your total cost of insurance between multiple options over the course of 1, 5, or even 10 years at your current rate, then factor in frequency of claims. For the same total coverage, all choices should statistically yield similar results; your choice of plan is simply a matter of your risk tolerance. Of course, nobody plans to have claims. If that were the case, then nobody would need insurance in the first place!

CHAPTER 5

Credit and Responsible Credit Use

What Is Credit and Why Is It Important?

On the surface, your credit score is a number that represents your perceived ability to borrow and pay back money. Notice the use of the word *perceived*; that is, the perception of this ability may be better or worse than your actual ability. This score ranges from 300 to 850, with 300 being "no bank is going to touch you with a 10-foot pole" and 850 being "you are the god of credit." This range is further broken down into five smaller buckets (Table 5.1).

Table 5.1 Credit score table

Score range	Rating
300–579	Poor
580–669	Fair
670–739	Good
740–799	Very good
800–850	Excellent

There is not a single score that will give you a certain interest rate or borrowing power, though your score will certainly impact the range for which you are eligible. This score is used in conjunction with the rest of your financial health to help banks determine what they are willing to lend to you and at what cost in the form of the interest rate. There is a much more detailed report called a credit report, which is a multi-page report that has all of your lending history, including current loan amounts and minimum payments, and past loan amounts such as old student loans. We will not discuss the credit report in detail, but you can get your credit reports for free once a year from each of the three major credit bureaus: Experian,[13] Equifax,[14] and TransUnion.[15] If you need a quick report on your credit, most credit card companies offer free FICO (Fair Isaac Corporation) score checks. Note that FICO calculates your score slightly differently than the credit bureaus, but it offers a quick gut check of your overall score. If you want a more detailed report and are out of free reports, you can purchase them through the credit bureaus for a small amount of money.

Facts About Credit and Credit Cards

- Credit cards are not inherently bad. Using credit cards to buy things that you cannot afford is bad.
- The reason why credit card interest is so high is that it is a form of unsecured loan: a loan that has no collateral. Houses and cars have relatively low interest rates because if you cannot pay the loan, the bank will repossess the vehicle or foreclose on the house. If you spend $100 at the bar on your credit card and can't pay that back, the credit card service provider has no way of recuperating even a portion of that value without sending you to collections.
- As mentioned, you should keep your credit locked until you are ready to open a new line of credit. You can lock your credit by registering with each of the credit bureaus and lock them individually. It takes only a few minutes and you are able to lock and unlock your credit an unlimited number of times for free. This will greatly reduce your risk of loan-based identity theft.
- Credit cards offer a layer of protection that debit cards and cash cannot provide. For instance, if someone steals and spends your cash using your debit card, that money is gone forever. If you file a police report and a fraud claim with your bank, it may take weeks or months to get your money back. You might not get it back at all. With a credit card, all you have to do is report fraud or theft to them, and they will reverse the transaction almost instantly. The credit card companies take on the risk so that you don't have to. This is another reason for the high interest rates.

- You are able to negotiate your fees and APY (annual percentage yield) by simply calling your creditor and telling them that you'd like to have an $XX annual fee or XX% annual rate because ABC creditor is offering you a new credit card and you're thinking of jumping ship. They are surprisingly willing to do a lot to help retain you, especially if you've been a loyal customer for a few years.
- Your credit card interest rate does not matter if you pay off your statement balance each month, as you should be doing every month. The first month of borrowing for any purchase is interest-free.
    - For example, you purchase something for $100 on June 5th and your statement starts and ends on the 20th of each month. On June 20th, you will receive a statement that shows all of your purchases from May 20 to June 20, including the $100 purchase. That statement balance will be due sometime in early to mid-July, say July 15th. If you pay off that $100 purchase and the rest of the statement balance by July 15th, you will not owe any interest on the money borrowed, no matter how much you spent in that period.
- A cash advance is when you use your credit card like a debit card, for example, withdrawing physical cash from an ATM. Typically this comes with a small percentage fee between 3% and 5% of the total withdrawal. For example, if you withdraw $1,000 from an ATM using your credit card cash advance and the fee is 4%, you will owe a $40 fee. This is obviously not ideal, but if you absolutely need cash and there is no physical bank around or if you don't have your debit card, it's not a terrible way to get it. Another way to get physical cash is to go to a store that offers cash back with purchases.

The Five Factors of Credit and How to Improve Them

Your credit score is determined by your performance in the following five categories:

1. Payment History (35%)
    a. This is based on whether you make your payments on time. Keep in mind that a late payment of a few days on your credit

card will not negatively impact your credit score. You have to be a full statement cycle late, generally 30 days, before your credit card will report a "late payment" toward your credit score. However, you will still be liable for the late fee even if you're only a couple days late.

b. Late fees are typically around $30 to $50 depending on the card company. If you have been diligent about paying your credit card on time for many years, you can usually get your late fee removed by calling your credit card company and asking them to remove it. It's not guaranteed, but it's worth a shot.

c. Late payments that have been reported to your credit stay on your report for 7 years, so it is imperative that you stay on top of your payments, even if it's just the minimum amount.

2. Amounts You Owe (30%)

a. Also known as revolving credit utilization rate, this is based on the amount that you currently owe as a percentage of the total amount you are allowed to borrow. For example, if your credit card balance was $1,500 last month and your total credit limit on all your credit cards is $25,000, your revolving credit is $1,500 / $25,000 × 100% = 6%.

b. A solid utilization to aim for is less than 30%, but some credit experts recommend keeping it as low as 10%.

c. Credit utilization does not have any memory, which means that if your credit score drops from having high utilization, it will go back up immediately the month after you pay it down.

d. Your credit has lower utilization the higher your credit limits are, so it is advantageous to always request credit limit increases as long as there is no hard pull on your credit. Additionally, it is also advantageous to keep old credit cards open as long as there is no annual fee and it's in a safe spot with no risk of theft.

3. Length of Credit History (15%)

a. This is the age of the oldest credit account that you have associated with your name and/or or the average age of all your active accounts.

b. This is another reason to keep your oldest credit card open. It is possible that a card company will close an inactive card, so if you have an old card that you don't use regularly, you may want to put a small recurring expense on it and let it autopay.

    i. For example, my first credit card was my Discover IT Chrome credit card for students with a $500 limit. It now has a $20,000 credit limit and the account is over 10 years old. It would be detrimental to close this account, but I have other cards that bring me more value based on my lifestyle. Therefore, I just pay for my monthly Spotify subscription with my Discover card and autopay the card with my checking account. The card physically sits in a drawer at home and not even in my wallet.

4. New Credit Inquiries (10%)

    a. If you are always inquiring about opening a new line of credit, lenders will view you as a riskier person who is at risk of not paying off current debts. Therefore, having many inquiries is a negative on credit score.

    b. There is a caveat: Many inquiries made within a small period of time (e.g., getting preapproved by multiple banks during a home- or car-buying process) will only count as one credit inquiry since they are grouped for a single purchase. Note that different credit score calculators use a different time period for these groupings. FICO uses 45 days while VantageScore uses a 14-day period. This is one of the many reasons why your credit score will vary from source to source.

    c. Hard versus soft inquiries: Hard inquiries occur when you are actively shopping for a loan or applying for credit cards. A few hard inquiries might ding your credit score by a few points, but remember that your credit is meant to be used! Soft inquiries are credit checks pulled for a rental application or work background check. They also occur when you request a credit limit increase on your credit cards. Soft credit checks do not affect credit scores.

    d. You do not want more than six total credit inquiries in a 2-year period. This is the upper limit at which banks will not lend to you anymore. Ideally, you want to keep inquiries to 3 to 5 in a 2-year period. One to two inquiries in a 2-year period are almost negligible on your credit report.

5. Types of Credit (10%)
    a. Having installment loans such as a car loan or even personal loan is generally seen as less risky than many revolving loans like credit cards. The number of loans you have also plays this role. Having many loans is not necessarily a bad thing as long as you are within your utilization rate.
    b. Of course, this means that you have to borrow money in order to have a credit score. This is one of the major drawbacks of credit scores and credit borrowing in general. Luckily, a simple credit card that you use for general expenses is enough to build credit.

Keep in mind that your credit score is dynamic and is only a small part of your financial health. Many people tend to want to keep their score as high as possible in exchange for never using their credit (e.g., not wanting a car dealership to pull credit to qualify you for a good financing deal because it will temporarily lower your credit score). Credit is a tool to be used as part of your financial arsenal. Do not aim for the highest credit score at the expense of other aspects of your financial health. In general, your ability to borrow money depends on both your credit and your income. An 820 credit score means nothing if you don't make enough money to pay the loan back. Your income and credit are both integral aspects of your borrowing power.

Caveat: Do not take out loans for the purpose of building credit. That is a common myth perpetuated by people who don't understand how credit works. Every loan you take out costs money in the form of interest. You should only use credit when needed or when it makes mathematical sense.

I Cannot Get Approved for a Credit Card—How Should I Proceed?

There are two primary methods: authorized users and/or secure credit cards.

Being an authorized user on another person's credit card is an excellent zero-effort way to build credit. In fact, you don't even need to have physical possession of the card! Here is an example: I have a great credit score, but my little cousin doesn't. I call my credit card company and state that I would like to add an authorized user (some allow you to do this through the app). They ask for my cousin's name and sometimes Social Security Number and then they issue a card. The card that is issued has their name on it, but it links to my account. Which means that the spending habits on your account will affect both persons' credit scores. The other person does not need to actually use the card at all. When my cousin goes to open his own credit card, he will be greeted with an excellent credit score and extensive credit history. You can do this with people of any age.

Secure credit cards are small balance credit cards that are backed by a collateral of your own deposit. For example, you can get a $500 limit credit card by placing a $500 deposit. The bank will provide you with a card to use that is able to pay up to $500. If you are unable to pay back the loan, the bank will keep your deposit. Once you show that you are capable of paying off the balance each month for several months, the bank will close your secured credit card, return your deposit, and issue you a standard credit card that has no deposit requirement. This is an excellent way to build credit without relying on another person.

Do NOT borrow money for the sake of building credit. I repeat. Do NOT borrow money for the sake of building credit. This is a huge financial misconception that many people grew up with and many people still perpetuate. You DO NOT need to finance a $30k car at 18% to build your credit right out of college. A loan like that, which is not uncommon for first-time borrowers with no credit, costs almost $50k after a 5-year period. You should ask yourself: Is having a higher credit score after 5 years worth $20k? Never in a million years. The methods listed earlier are zero-cost ways to build credit. Did I mention that you DO NOT need to borrow money for the sake of building your credit score? Anybody who tells you to borrow money to build credit automatically discredits themselves financially, and you should never take financial advice from that person ever again.

If you are unable to secure a loan on your own, you may be asked to bring a cosigner. A cosigner is someone who you bring in to back your loan using their credit. They are equally as responsible for the loan as you are. If you stop paying your loan, your cosigner is responsible to pick up the payments; otherwise, both persons' credit scores will suffer. If you are ever asked to cosign something, be aware that you will be 100% on the hook if that person ever chooses not to pay their loan anymore. Do not cosign for anything that you are not 100% comfortable assuming the loan for.

Building a Loan Amortization Schedule

A huge loan misconception is "all of the early payments go toward interest" and "the bank charges you more money up front because they want their money now." While that can be how it appears, it all comes down to a math exercise: the loan amortization.

A loan amortization schedule is a table that shows the breakdown of what portion of your payment goes to interest and what portion goes to principal when paying back a loan. Most loans have consistent payments through the loan term, so naturally, as the principal decreases, the amount paid to interest decreases while the principal payoff is accelerated. The amount that you pay in interest for any particular payment period is based on your interest rate and how much principal you have left to pay off, that is, the outstanding loan balance.

Consider a $100,000 loan with a 6% interest rate. Unless stated otherwise, 6% is the *annual* rate; thus, your *monthly* interest rate will be 6% / 12 = 0.5%. In your first month, you will owe the bank $100,000 $\times$ 0.5% = $500 in interest. If you only pay the bank $500, the amount that you owe will not decrease. You must pay interest plus some principal in order to decrease your balance. The amount that you pay toward the principal will be determined by the loan term. Let's use a 5-year term as an example, which leads to a monthly payment of:

$$\text{PMT} = \frac{\dfrac{i}{n} \cdot P}{1 - \left(1 + \dfrac{i}{n}\right)^{-n \cdot t}} \Rightarrow \frac{\left(\dfrac{0.06}{12}\right) \cdot 100{,}000}{1 - \left(1 + \dfrac{0.06}{12}\right)^{-12 \cdot 5}} = \$1933.28$$

Note that the interest portion of the monthly payment is your monthly interest rate multiplied by the remaining balance on the loan.

Interest	Principal	Total Payment	Remaining Balance
$I_N = \dfrac{P_N \cdot i}{n}$	$P_N = PMT - I_N$	$PMT = \dfrac{\frac{i}{n} \cdot P_{total}}{1 - (1 + \frac{i}{n})^{-nt}}$	$B_N = B_{N-1} - P_{N-1}$

Figure 5.1 Loan amortization formulas

N = payment number, n = number of payments per year, t = loan term
(years), i = interest rate (decimal), P = original principal

From here, we can use this monthly payment to develop the amortization schedule (Figure 5.1).

If you want to build your own amortization schedule in Excel or Google Sheets, you may want to include columns for the Accumulated Equity and Total Interest, which is the sum of all the principal and interest paid thus far, respectively. You may also want to include a running loan-to-value ratio (LTV ratio), which is the current loan balance divided by the original loan amount. If you plan on making lump sum payments toward your loan, you can manually input them by changing the principal column to include an additional payment amount. Alternatively, you can add an additional column and subtract the value of the additional payment column from the remaining balance each month.

If you don't like the nasty formula for total payment, you may find the PMT function useful in Excel/Google Sheets:

=PMT(rate/(# of periods per year), # of periods per year × years, starting balance)

[Note that starting balance must be a negative number]

For a 30-year $320k loan at 7% interest, the resulting graph is shown in Figure 5.2.

If you hate spreadsheets and math (how dare you), you can see a premade amortization calculator in the "Basic Loan Amortization" tab in the shared spreadsheet.

With any loan, you can get this amortization table from your loan officer or equivalent financial representative. It is always beneficial to play

30-Year Loan Amortization

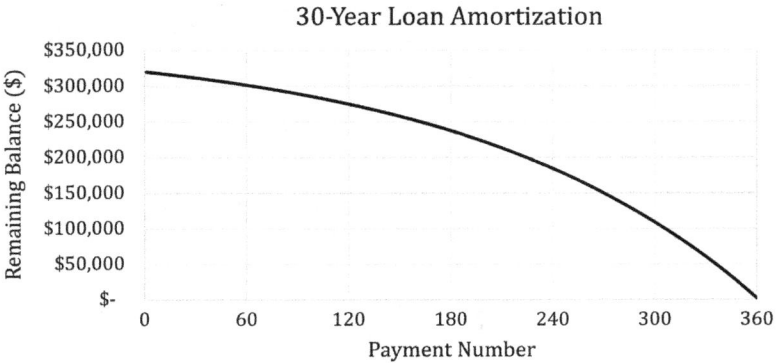

Figure 5.2 30-year loan amortization graph

Shows how slow your progress is at the beginning of the loan term, but quickly accelerates toward the end as the balance shrinks.

around with your own table before signing any papers so you know exactly how much money you are paying for something and how changing different factors might affect you. For example, some car dealerships offer 0% financing for vehicles if you have excellent credit, but if you don't qualify for 0%, they might give you $2,000 off the MSRP (manufacturer's suggested retail price) of the car in exchange for a 5% interest rate. With an amortization table, you can see the exact difference. The numbers in this sheet are large and scary, but reading the section on the Cost of Capital may help put your mind at ease when borrowing large amounts of money for long periods of time!

CHAPTER 6

Paying Off Debt

Rather than thinking of debt as borrowing from an entity, think of debt as borrowing from your future self with the entity helping you do that for a cost (interest). Not all debt is bad. It can enable us to buy homes or invest in businesses without having all the cash up front. In this section, however, we will be focusing on the bad kinds of debt that typically come in the form of credit cards or personal loans. You may have taken loans to go to school that yielded a job with income that does not justify the cost—that would technically be considered bad debt. In a broader sense, any debt that keeps you awake at night or makes your blood pressure go up is bad debt.

The Different Types of Loans

There is a myriad of different types of loans you can take, from a basic credit card to student loans, business loans, or even payday loans. There are several key differences between them, from what type of asset, if any, backs them, to what the repayment requirements are. This is not an exhaustive list.

- Secured Versus Unsecured Loans
  - Secured loans are backed by an asset, such as a house or car. They typically have lower interest rates than unsecured loans since the lender can reclaim the asset in the event of failure to pay. Secured loans typically require down payments in case the value of the asset drops below the purchase price. If that occurs, that loan is said to be underwater.
  - If you are underwater on a vehicle, you will owe the difference between the loan amount and the vehicle value in the event that you sell the vehicle or the vehicle is destroyed. Therefore,

you may want to consider purchasing gap insurance, which will cover the difference between the amount owed and the value of the car in the event of an accident where the vehicle is totaled. The recommended alternative is putting a larger down payment. Gap insurance does not come into play when selling an underwater vehicle.

- Fixed Versus Variable Interest Loans
  - Most loans are fixed-interest loans, which, as the name implies, carry the same interest rate throughout the life of the loan. There are certain scenarios where a variable interest loan would be beneficial. Variable interest loans have the ability to change rates over the life of the loan.
  - Credit cards can also be variable rate. Some cards advertise their rate as the prime rate plus some add-on rate. For example, if the prime rate is 5% and the credit card add-on rate is 15%, then your total credit card rate is 20%. The prime rate[16] is the rate set by the Federal Reserve. The additional 15% is charged by the credit card company for taking on risk.
- Interest-Only Loans
  - This loan is exactly what it sounds like: a loan on which you pay only interest and not principal. This loan is useful in a situation where you need to purchase a home that you know you will not live in for a long time, such as a live-in flip home. Rather than putting money into the principal of the home, you opt to pay interest only. When you sell the house, all the money from the sale will go to pay off the loan balance. It seems silly, but consider that the principal part of a mortgage is essentially a piggy bank that you're forced to contribute to and have virtually zero access to. Home equity is mathematically indifferent than having that same sum of cash in a savings account, except you can take the money out of your savings any time you'd like with no fees.
- Balloon Loans
  - These are loans that do not reach the full amortization period. They offer lower monthly payments in exchange for a lump sum being paid at the end of the loan term. This loan also has

very specific uses, such as in fix-and-flip real estate; the buyer uses a balloon loan over a 3-year period and fixes up the home. The payments are low and when the renovations are complete, they sell the property and use a part of the proceeds to pay off the loan.

Beware: Payday Loans

These are typically loans that have short terms like a few weeks, or until your next paycheck, like the name implies. There is nothing beneficial about these loans, and the interest rates are astronomical. Recall that interest rates are annual, meaning a 5% interest rate would mean a 5% charge over a year. However, payday loans don't represent the interest rate in this way. Because of the short loan terms, many desperate borrowers don't even know the true interest rate.

For example, you get a payday loan for $1,000. You return the money in 2 weeks with $50 interest. That doesn't sound too bad, until you annualize the interest amount. A payment of $50 per 2 weeks is $1,300/year in interest. This means that your actual interest rate is 130%!

Do not, under any circumstances, consider a payday loan. They are predatory and very hard to recover from.

Calculating Your Debt-to-Income Ratio (DTI)

Your DTI is similar to your credit utilization ratio. While your credit utilization ratio is how much you are currently borrowing relative to how much you are able to borrow, your DTI is how much of your gross income goes to paying off debt. The easiest way to think about this is on a monthly basis. In its most basic form, your DTI is your minimum monthly payments on all of your loans (and legal obligations like rent or child support) divided by your monthly gross income. Let's say you make $5,000/month and you have the following payments: $1,200 mortgage/rent, $400 car, $100 minimum credit card payments, and $300 student loans. Your total debt is $2,000, which makes your total DTI 2,000/5,000 = 40%.

Typically, a good DTI is under 36%. You should have no problem finding additional loans at this level. Between 36% and 50%, it gets increasingly difficult to borrow money. When you get to the higher end, you may find yourself with drastically higher interest rates than at the lower end. Above 50% and almost no banks will loan to you. When purchasing a home, a lender will use your DTI to determine the maximum amount you can afford for a house and put your cap at around 42%.

Refinancing Debt

When you obtain a loan, you pay it off over some period of time at the agreed-upon interest rate. However, if you have access to borrowed funds at a lower interest rate, you can use those funds to pay off your higher interest debt. This is called refinancing. Typically, you refinance an existing loan with a loan from another bank. There may be underwriting fees, which is essentially paperwork that is done by the bank to set up the loan. Refinance underwriting fees vary from $0 for student loans to hundreds of dollars for car loans, or even thousands of dollars for mortgage refinancing.

Calculating your payback period is fairly straightforward. Let's say that you have a $30k car loan for 48 months and 6% interest. An online calculator can tell you that the monthly payment is $702/month. Refinancing your loan to 4% might cost around $200. Your new payment would be $676/month, a savings of $26/month. Your payback period is $200 / ($26/month) = 8 months. Whether the effort of refinancing is worth it is up to you! $26 is a nonzero amount of money, but it is objectively not a huge amount. You might simply opt to pay off your loan faster instead of refinancing, yet another example of the "personal" part of personal finance.

Snowball Versus Avalanche

There are two main approaches to paying off debt, but you may find yourself using a combination of the two. Paying off debt is a great way to improve your financial health and get a guaranteed rate of return on the cash that you're putting in!

Consider the following list of debts:

- $1,000 on a Discover credit card (25% interest, minimum payment $30/month)
- $5,000 on a Chase credit card (20% interest, minimum payment $100/month)
- $8,000 student loan #1 (6% interest, minimum payment $90/month)
- $2,000 student loan #2 (5% interest, minimum payment $25/month)
- $10,000 car loan (7% interest, minimum payment $200/month)

Total debt: $26,000
Total minimum payments: $445/month

Let's discuss how to tackle these debts with different methods!

The **avalanche** method is done by paying the loan with the highest interest rate first while paying the minimum payment on all the other loans. Mathematically, this is the most optimal method to pay off debt since you are spending the least amount of time with higher interest loans and prolonging lower interest loans, thus lowering total interest paid. After the highest interest loan is paid off, you can move onto the loan with the next highest interest rate while continuing to pay the minimum on all the other loans. You repeat this process until all debts are paid off. Using the aforementioned numbers, the order for avalanche method would be:

1. Discover credit card (25%)
2. Chase credit card (20%)
3. Car loan (7%)
4. Student loan #1 (6%)
5. Student loan #2 (5%)

The **snowball** method may not be the mathematically optimal solution, but it can be the psychologically optimal solution. The snowball method is when you pay the debt with the smallest balance first and then take the payment from that debt and roll it into the next smallest debt. You do this while paying the minimum on everything else. You are essentially paying off the smallest loan more quickly and then allocating the monthly payment from that loan to the next smallest loan. At this point, you have eliminated one monthly payment and diverted it to the next loan. Although it is not mathematically efficient, it gives you a greater sense of accomplishment by paying off small loans first. It is also a faster way of freeing up cash flow by reducing the minimum monthly payments and thereby improving your DTI ratio. Using the aforementioned numbers, the order for snowball method would be:

1. Discover credit card ($1,000)
2. Student loan #2 ($2,000)
3. Chase credit card ($5,000)
4. Student loan #1 ($8,000)
5. Car loan ($10,000)

You may choose to use a combination of these methods if your interest rates are relatively similar. In the case of this example, there are two distinct groups of debt—high-interest unsecured debt, and relatively low-interest debt. Therefore, it may be advantageous to use a hybrid of both the snowball and avalanche methods.

1. Discover credit card: No doubt this one has to go first; it's the highest interest rate and lowest balance
2. Chase credit card: Next highest interest by a long shot
3. Student loan #2: This is because the interest rate between loan #1 and loan #2 is not significant enough to make a huge impact, but paying off the $2,000 loan first will allow you to shovel all your money into student loan #1 or car loan while much more easily closing out student loan #2
4. Car loan: This has a slightly higher interest rate, but is backed by a depreciating asset. Car loan terms are generally shorter than student loan terms, so knocking this one out first will allow you to focus all of your energy on student loan #1.
5. Student Loan #1.

Discussion: As you can see, there is a way to combine the mathematical optimizations of the avalanche method with the psychological wins of the snowball method. No matter which method you choose, even if it's hybrid, you will be golden as long as you follow your plan.

Alternative Methods to Paying Off Debt

There are a few last-resort methods to get rid of high-interest debt. Generally, these methods are not so much about getting rid of debt but, instead, about shuffling it around so it's more manageable. Some examples include balance transfers to 0% credit cards, loans on their 401(k),[17] or taking out a personal loan. This is mathematically efficient because they transfer debt from a high-interest account to one with lower or no interest, making it easier to pay off more quickly. Note that credit card companies that offer 0% interest on balance transfers typically charge a small percentage up front of the amount that is being transferred, usually 3% to 5%, similar rates to a cash advance.

While mathematically more efficient than keeping high-interest credit card debt, they are psychologically inefficient. Above all else, the person who holds the debt needs to fix the problems that got them into debt in the first place. Moving the balance from one place to another isn't going to help if the original credit card begins racking up a balance again. Although it can be extremely helpful to some people, many people find themselves in a worse position than they were before when using these methods. If you are going to use any of the methods, you need to ensure that you will not increase your debt again. This means revisiting your budget and spending then cutting up your credit cards if you choose to go this route.

Scott's Thoughts: Debt Philosophy

My personal philosophy of the 5% rule depends on the debt type.

My personal threshold is generally 6%. The reason is that even though you get a guaranteed return of 5% for paying off 5% interest debt, there is a price for flexibility. Even if I have debt at 6%, I might opt to keep liquid cash in a high-yield account until I can pay it off in full. While technically I will be paying slightly more interest, I give myself the flexibility to have cash on hand to use for other things. Here is an example of when this philosophy benefited me:

> I had low-interest student loans (<6%). I was putting aside cash in a HYSA to pay off student loans in chunks so I could maintain extra cash on hand. I was planning on paying off the higher interest loans in full once I had accumulated enough cash to do so. However, my 18-year-old car decided to die so I went shopping for another used car. The car was $32k out the door, and out of curiosity, I asked the dealer what the interest rate would be to finance it. They said 9% even with excellent credit. I said "screw that" and paid cash for the car. Even though I burned my student loan fund on a car, I avoided a 9% loan because I had the flexibility.

On the contrary, I dislike low-interest debt in the long term because it increases overall risk in the event of job loss. Most debt must be paid even when unemployed. My low-interest student loan minimum payment was $550/month, which meant my 6-month emergency fund needed to have an extra $3,300 to cover that payment. It raised my baseline expenses all around. Therefore, I still contributed extra each month to knock it out as quickly as possible. I recognize that I was extremely fortunate to be able to throw money at a low-interest loan in the first place; many early-career folks do not have that luxury. Even if I hypothetically had an investment property with a 6% interest rate on the mortgage, I would still prioritize my 4% student loans over the property. The reason is that the investment property makes money and has tax advantages. My student loans were not bringing me a tangible benefit other than a monthly payment, and keeping them around longer was not going to make my degree worth more. Note that student loan interest is tax deductible but only below a certain income. In summary, how you manage debt versus cash reserves can be very personal. Nonetheless, there is no better feeling than being debt free, no matter the interest rate!

Pay Off Debt Versus Invest

Understanding the 5% threshold for debt payoff versus investing (from Step 3 of the Personal Finance Flowchart): The historical market return over the last 30 years is 10.5%. Accounting for inflation of 2.5%, the amount is about 8%. After paying 20% in long-term capital gains taxes on your return on investment, you are at 6.4%. However, this return is not guaranteed while debt payoff rate of return is guaranteed, so you can round it down another 1% for the "guarantee factor." Note that there are loans that may be above 5% that are worth holding for a longer period of time such as mortgages, since interest on mortgages is tax deductible if you itemize your taxes.

In general, any high-interest debt of above 5% is worth paying off sooner rather than later. See Section "Why Is 5% the Threshold for Paying Off Debt versus Investing" in the appendix for a detailed example demonstrating the difference between saving and paying off debt.

Despite there being mathematical reasons for having 5% as a threshold for paying off debt, you may want to pay off debt even if it is less than 5% interest. It's suboptimal, yes, but few people ever regret paying off debt even if it is considered lower interest. Paying off debt also frees up cash flow by eliminating a minimum monthly payment from your budget and improves your DTI ratio, which will improve your credit score and other things like homebuying power. Note that after paying off a loan balance your credit score might drop temporarily since you closed an account, but typically your score will rebound within a month or two. If you have leftover cash at the end of the month after completing the personal finance flowchart, you may want to consider paying a portion of it into low-interest debt even though it isn't mathematically optimal.

Ultimately, your psychology will be what dictates your appetite for holding onto debt, regardless of the interest rate. As mentioned, a suboptimal choice might be the best choice if it helps you sleep better at night!

CHAPTER 7

Taxes

"Nothing is certain except death and taxes"—Ben Franklin. The more you understand taxes, the more you will be able to optimize your asset allocation and make informed decisions about what to do with your hard-earned money! In this section, we will cover the basics of taxes and debunk some common myths.

Basic Tax Terminology

- Taxable Event: Aside from income you gain from selling your time (i.e., your job), there are many other things that are taxable. To understand this better, it is easier to think of events as "taxable" or "nontaxable."
  - Taxable events include but are not limited to selling an investment for a profit, selling a home for a profit, getting paid to babysit, flipping furniture for a profit, or collecting (non-qualified) dividends from an investment.
  - Nontaxable events that are commonly mistaken for taxable events include when your investments skyrocket and you have not sold them, resulting in a high net worth (common mistake when people say "tax the rich").
  - Note that even if you experience a taxable event, your taxes incurred may be zero depending on the law (e.g., sale of a home for up to $250k in profit if lived in for more than 24 of the last 60 months).
- Progressive Tax System: Where taxes go up as you earn incrementally more money; that is, the next dollar you earn is taxed at a higher rate than the current dollar earned. Earning more does not put your entire income in the next tax bracket.

- Regressive Tax System: Where taxes go down as you earn incrementally more money; that is, the next dollar you earn is taxed at a lower rate than the current dollar earned. Earning more does not put your entire income in the lower tax bracket.
- Marginal Tax Bracket: Your federal taxes are broken up into income segments. Your marginal rate means that only the income that falls into that bracket is subject to that tax rate, not your entire income. Table 7.1 best summarizes the income brackets for single filers (as of 2025). Note that the marginal tax system used for federal taxes is a progressive tax system.
- Federal Insurance Contributions Acts (FICA): These taxes are in addition to federal income tax and include Social Security[18] and Medicare Tax.[19] The amount is 15.3%, although your W2 employer covers half of that amount, or 7.65%. Self-employed folks and independent contractors are on the hook for the full 15.3%. These also have brackets, albeit a bit larger than the federal taxes. Note that the FICA tax is a regressive tax since it gets lower once you reach a certain income level (Table 7.2).

Table 7.1 2025 federal income tax for single filers

Tax rate (%)	Taxable income	Taxes owed
10	$0–$11,925	10% of your income
12	$11,926–$48,475	$1,192.50 plus 12% of the amount over $11,925
22	$48,476–$103,350	$5,578.50 plus 22% of the amount over $48,475
24	$103,351–$197,300	$17,651 plus 24% of the amount over $103,350
32	$197,301–$250,525	$40,199 plus 32% of the amount over $197,300
35	$250,526–$626,350	$57,231 plus 35% of the amount over $250,525
37	$626,351 and above	$188,769.75 plus 37% of the amount over $626,350

Table 7.2 2025 social security taxes for single filers

Tax rate (%)	Taxable income	Notes
6.20	$0–$176,100	Social Security Tax (employer pays another 6.2%)
1.45	All wages subject to tax	Medicare Tax (employer pays another 1.45%)
0.90	$200,000 and above	Additional Medicare Tax for high earners

- Deduction: A reduction to your taxable income. These can be in the form of 401(k), Health Savings Account (HSA) contributions, mortgage interest, and property tax, but can also be in the form of business expenses if you are an independent contractor. You can also take deductions such as the "standard deduction," which is a predetermined deduction that the IRS will allow you to take in lieu of your itemized deductions.
  - Example 1: Your gross income is $60k. You decide to contribute $10k to your pretax 401(k) and use the IRS standard deduction of $15k. Your taxable income is now $60k − $10k − $15k = $35k, which puts you in the 12% federal tax bracket.
  - Example 2: You mow lawns for rich people and make $200k/year in revenue. However, you incur business expenses such as your truck, trailer, mowing equipment, fuel and maintenance, and a helper, which all cost you $110k/year total. Therefore, your taxable income is $200k − $110k = $90k/year.
- Write-Off: When you take a deduction that is a capital loss, it is considered a write-off. For example, if you go to the grocery store and accidentally drop a carton of eggs before checking out, you won't have to pay for it and the grocery store will simply "write it off" as a loss. This will count as a business loss for the grocery store and thereby reduce taxable income of the store owner.
  - Note that a write-off is still a loss. Do not believe people when they say, "It's ok it was a write-off." You still incur the loss of value. Like a deduction, you will never reduce your tax burden by the amount of the write-off.
- Cost Basis: The cost basis of an asset is a way to describe what you will use when calculating the profit when sold. While it is usually the purchase price of the asset, this is not always the case. Consider the following example:
  - You purchase a house for $100k and spend $20k on renovations. The $20k increased your *cost basis* to $120k. Therefore, if you were to sell the condo for $130k, your profit would be $130k − ($100k + $20k) = $10k.

○ Let's say you decide not to sell the house and you rent it out for 5 years while taking $10k *depreciation* each year. While taking depreciation reduces taxable income year to year, it also decreases your cost basis to $120k − 5 × $10k = $70k. You now decide to sell it after it has appreciated to $160k. Your capital gain on the sale is $160k − $70k = $90k.

- Capital Gain/Loss: A capital gain or loss is a gain or loss that originates from the sale of an asset, whether that be a used couch, stocks, a home, or a product. The act of "selling" something is considered a taxable event, whether you made or lost money. If you made money, you are subject to capital gains taxes; if you lost money, you may be able to deduct your losses to offset capital gains and thereby potentially reducing your tax burden.

- Short-Term Investment: A short-term investment is generally one you've held for less than 1 year. Short-term capital gains are taxed as ordinary income (as if you were paid more at work). Typically, the taxes on short-term investments are higher than on long-term investments.

- Long-Term Investment: A long-term investment is generally one you've held for more than a year. The taxes paid on this are in different brackets than your ordinary earned income, but the brackets themselves are based on your taxable income. See Table 7.3 for the 2025 brackets.

- Tax Withholding or Withholding Tax: You may come across this phrase on your pay stub or elsewhere. Many people confuse this with tax liability. When your company pays you, they withhold taxes to pay the government/state. That amount varies from person to person due to factors such as pretax deductions, property

Table 7.3 *2025 long-term capital gains tax for single filers*

Tax rate (%)	Taxable income	Notes
0	$0–$47,025	If your income is in the described range, you are obligated to pay that percentage of your net long-term capital gains in taxes
15	$47,026–$518,900	
20	$518,901 and above	

tax, and mortgage interest or tax credits such as childcare tax credit, EV tax credit, and so on. Therefore, the withholding is simply an estimate. *It is not how much you pay in taxes.* When you file your taxes with the IRS, your taxes are adjusted via a tax return, or a tax payment. Your W4 form[20] determines your withholding, and you can request an adjustment from your company at any time by resubmitting the form.

Common Tax Myths

- "I will take home less money if my paycheck is in the next tax bracket."
  - Only the income above the threshold is taxed at the higher marginal rate, not your entire income. You will never take home less pay after making more money. This is one of the biggest tax misconceptions. You will pay more in taxes, but the incremental tax increase will never exceed your increase in income. Many people turn down raises because they believe that they will take home less money if their salary increase pushes them into the next tax bracket.
- "Don't worry, it's a write-off."
  - This phrase is commonly used by people who are able to take business deductions. They believe that they will take home more money by purchasing a work truck or another large business expense.
  - Example: Let's say your marginal federal tax rate is 24%. You spend $100k on a truck (this is not uncommon—a Ford F-250 Platinum Diesel is $90k+). You will be able to write off $100k, which will save you approximately $24k in taxes, but after you have spent $100k. It's like using a coupon for 24% off to buy something you didn't even need in the first place!
- "Having a large tax return is good."
  - During tax season, many people are very happy to find that they will be getting large tax returns. In reality, the amount that you are being taxed has nothing to do with what you get back on your return and everything to do with how much

you made and withheld in that business year. In fact, if you receive a large tax return, it means that your withholding (see W4 form) was too high and you essentially just gave the government an interest-free loan! Another way to think about it is that you have placed money into a 0% interest savings account that you have no access to until you do your taxes. The money you receive back on a tax return was rightfully yours to begin with.

- What is far more important than your tax return is your overall tax burden. That number is the total dollar amount in taxes that you pay in the tax year after you file your taxes. That is the only number that matters. Your tax return is either a "feel good" or "feed bad" number—it has no bearing on how much tax you are paying.

- "Getting paid in cash means you don't have to pay taxes on it."
  - While cash is not automatically tracked like credit card transactions, it is still considered taxable income. Many businesses do shady things under the table with cash, but that doesn't make it legal. The same idea applies to gains from cryptocurrency since it is also not tracked by the government.
  - The biggest legal benefit to paying with cash is that the establishment does not have to pay the credit card transaction fees, which can take away a sizable portion of profits for small transactions. This is why there are minimum purchase amounts for cards at smaller establishments.

- "Don't gift me too much money or else I'll have to pay taxes on it."
  - The annual gift tax reporting limit is often confused with the lifetime tax limit. The annual *reporting* limit is $19,000 for 2025, which means that you simply need to report a gift exceeding that amount via IRS form 709. If you don't report that as a gift, then technically you would have to pay taxes on it. As long as you report gifts exceeding $19,000 and you are not approaching the lifetime gift limit, you will not owe taxes on gift amounts. The lifetime gift allowance is $13.99M. If you believe you will come remotely close to that amount in gifts,

you should contact a CPA because there are likely other tax implications you should be aware of.

- "Bonuses are taxed higher than my normal paycheck."
  - Bonuses are taxed like ordinary income, but when they are paid out there is a standard withholding tax of 22% (37% for any amount over $1M). The reason for this is that your normal paycheck has already accounted for all of the tax brackets below the federal tax bracket that you are currently in; therefore, your entire bonus will be taxed at whatever federal tax bracket you are in currently (remember that the withholding is simply an estimate).

Basic Tax Calculations

The effect of a deduction:

It's 2025 and you make $60k/year from your stuffed animal repair business. Your federal tax burden, based on the table in the "Marginal Tax Bracket" section, is $5,578.50 + 22% of the amount over $48,475, which is $2,535.50. Your total federal income tax burden is $8,114. Additionally, you will owe 15.3% FICA tax in the amount of $9,180 (if you are a W2 employee, you only owe half of the FICA tax—7.65%). Your total tax burden is $17,294, or 28.8% of your gross income, assuming no local or state taxes.

However, you decide to take some deductions to help reduce your *federal* tax burden. Let's look:

- The Standard Deduction[21] of $15,000, which reduces taxable income to $45,000.
- You contribute the full amount to your Traditional IRA of $7,000, which further reduces taxable income to $38,000.

Let's redo the tax calculations with a $38,000 net income after deductions:

Your FICA tax burden remains the same at $9,180. Your federal tax burden is $1,192.50 + 12% of the amount over $11,925, which is $3,129. Your total federal tax burden is $4,321.50 and your total tax burden is $13,501.50. This is 22.5% of your gross income.

Taking $22,000 worth of deductions resulted in $3,792.50 of savings or approximately 17% of the value of your deductions.

If you believe you have more deductions than the standard deduction, then you can itemize them. For example, you can deduct mortgage interest, property tax, or any business expenses related to the business. This only makes financial sense if the sum of these deductions exceeds the standard deduction. Other deductions such as pretax 401(k) contributions and student loan interest can be made in addition to the standard deduction.

In effect, the money that you save via a deduction is approximately the amount of the deduction multiplied by your marginal federal tax rate.

Common Tax Deductions

- Standard Deduction: This is the standard amount that you can deduct off your gross income as tax free. You can choose to take the Standard Deduction or Itemized Deductions. The Standard Deduction in 2025 is $15,000 per person for a single filer. In other words, if you earn $50,000 per year, your federal tax calculations will be calculated based on $35,000 per year ($50,000 − $15,000).
- Property Tax: The amount you pay as property tax on your home is already a tax; therefore, the IRS allows you to take a deduction in the amount paid.
- Mortgage Interest: Similar to property tax, you receive a tax deduction on interest or mortgage points paid in that calendar year. It is easy to see how owning a home might help you reduce your tax burden, but note that your property tax and mortgage interest paid must exceed the standard deduction for it to be worthwhile. As mentioned earlier, you will never save as much in taxes as you've paid in property tax and mortgage interest.
- Student Loan Interest: If your modified adjusted gross income (MAGI[22]) is below a certain threshold, you are eligible to deduct up to $2,500 per year off your gross income.
- Home Office: If you use a portion of your home for business purposes, you may be eligible to deduct a portion of your rent or

mortgage. Most people calculate this based on the square footage of their home office. Unless you have a massive office, this deduction turns out to be quite small. Nonetheless, it is still money back in your pocket if you are a small business owner!

- Mileage: If you drive for work (not a commute) as realtor or delivery driver, for example, you are eligible to deduct mileage. While some people choose to deduct based on the actual expenses of their vehicles, the IRS makes it simple by offering a flat rate per mile to deduct. In 2025, the mileage deduction is $0.70 per mile. For example, if you drove 1,000 miles this year for business purposes, you can deduct $700 from your gross income.

Most young professionals who don't own homes or have businesses end up taking the standard deduction, but some tax deductions, such as student loan interest, home office, and mileage, can be taken *in addition* to the standard deduction. Other deductions such as property tax and mortgage interest deductions are taken in lieu of the standard deduction. The full list of deductions can be found on the IRS website.

Tax Credits

A more direct impact on your tax burden is a tax credit. Unlike a tax deduction, which lowers your taxable income, a tax credit directly lowers your tax burden. For example, if you have children and earn under $200,000 per year ($400,000 if filing jointly), you are eligible for a tax credit for each child who meets the IRS requirements. Other tax credits are clean vehicle credits or clean home energy credits that you receive as "bonuses" for helping the environment! There are countless tax credits in existence, so be sure to do your research to see which ones you qualify for in any given year. Most tax software will ask you the relevant questions to see if you qualify, but you should do your own research too.

Filing Your Taxes

Filing your own taxes is much easier than most people make it seem. In most situations, hiring a pro will not get you more money back than doing it yourself. The amount of money that you pay in taxes is based on how much you make and your current tax situation. Hiring a tax professional does not change any of these circumstances. If you have a complicated tax situation, your tax professional may be more knowledgeable about certain permitted deductions, tax breaks, or organizational strategies to help you pay less in taxes, but for most young professionals the tax code is standard across the board.

Here are some examples of when to go to a CPA for professional help. If you meet one or more of these requirements, you should consider going to a professional:

- You have a small business (LLC, S-corp, etc.).
- You have rental properties.
- You received one-off income from sources that don't necessarily provide formal tax documentation (crypto sale, inheritance, life insurance, etc.).
- You had a life event such as marriage or selling a house.

Note that even if you meet any of the listed criteria, you still may not need to hire a CPA to do your taxes, but it would be worth it to consult with a CPA around the implications of your actions. Of course, when in doubt, you should always consult a tax professional. The key takeaway of this section is that hiring a professional to do your taxes does not always get you more money back, especially given the cost of hiring one.

CHAPTER 8

Investments: Putting Your Money to Work

What Is an Investment?

An investment is a place or entity where you set your money to generate a return to be collected in the future. In other words, you are paying your future self! While debt is borrowing from your future self to pay your current self, investing is your future self borrowing from your present self. There are many types of investments: stocks, bonds, mutual funds, index funds, businesses, real estate, crypto, or even baseball cards and antique furniture (hey, nobody said they had to be *good* investments!). The type of investments you choose to have in your portfolio should reflect your risk tolerance, desired level of return and involvement, and personal interest/expertise. For example, someone who has no interest in managing a property or knowledge in simple home repairs should not invest in real estate because it is a very hands-on investment that requires a niche skillset! That said, this section will focus on investments in the stock and bond markets. These investments tend to be the lowest maintenance/involvement and most popular over the last century.

Side note: You can also invest in yourself by completing certifications to increase your pay at work or going to training to increase your career skills. These are naturally difficult to quantify, but they are indeed investments. You can spend money to complete an MBA program that might earn you an extra $40k per year! However, this section will focus on *securities* rather than self-investments.

Do I Need a Financial Adviser?

If you are a young professional reading this book, the answer is probably no. Here is why: A financial adviser is someone who can help you achieve your financial goals and understand what's best for you based on your lifestyle, savings rates, and investment risk tolerance. You can easily learn how to do that on your own, mainly by reading books like these. Most people don't make enough money to need someone to manage their money for them, and any monetary gains received from such a financial optimization will be spent on hiring the adviser. Learning how to manage your own money is an incredibly valuable skill and can save you tens or hundreds of thousands of dollars over your life. Not only will you be more self-aware in your day-to-day finances, but you will also retain the costs of paying someone else to manage them for you.

Note on financial advisers: There are many different types of "financial advisers." The type that you want to look out for is called a fee-only *fiduciary financial adviser*,[23] which is an adviser who legally must act in your best interest and not their best interest. You want a fee-only adviser so you understand what you are paying up front versus a commission-based adviser who takes a percentage of your portfolio each year.

Financial advisers make money off your ignorance of financial management. As a result, many make it seem complicated to get started in investing or financial management. However, investing is not hard at all. You can make your portfolio as simple and hands-off as you'd like and still achieve your financial goals. There isn't anything a financial adviser can do for you that you can't learn from a book or on the Internet. Some situations in which a financial adviser is typically recommended is if you have an extremely complicated investment portfolio, have a large inheritance/cash windfall, are trying to set up a trust (get a lawyer to help for this too), are working toward a very specific financial goal, or are a top 1% earner. Statistically, none of the situations likely apply to you. Even if they did, a fiduciary Certified Financial Planner (CFP[24]) who charges by the hour may be your best option, even if it's a few hundred dollars an hour. You may think that a few hundred dollars an hour is a ridiculous rate—until you see the math in the following section.

The Cost of a Percent-Based Financial Adviser

The cost of hiring a financial adviser is usually a percentage of your portfolio amount, typically around 1%. If your portfolio or *assets under management* (AUM) is around $100k, your annual management fee would be around $1,000. This may not seem like a lot of money for now, but let's run the numbers over the long term. Let's say you are a high enough earner to justify using a financial adviser who charges 1% of AUM. You save $50k/year and your adviser invests it and earns a market average of 8% annually but takes 1% each year. In reality, you are earning 7%. Over 35 years, your balance is $6.91M. Pretty sweet.

Let's say you pocket the 1% and earn the full 8% on your investments. Your ending amount is $8.62M. Your last year of fees will be over 80 THOUSAND dollars, and your financial adviser cost you a total of $1.71M over 35 years, or about $49k per year on average. If somebody paid you $49k/year to spend 2 hours a week learning how to manage your own money, would you do it? By the way, 2 hours a week for a year for $49k works out to around $470/hour—talk about being your own financial consultant!

Naturally, your next question is, "Isn't my financial adviser going to be better than I am at investing my money?" The short answer is no. It is extremely rare that even professional investors consistently beat the market, and picking one that does is just as random as picking which team is going to win Monday night football. You can look at all the stats you want on the game, but at the end of the day your guess will be as good as anyone's. If that weren't the case, there would be a lot more millionaires from sports betting, but that is simply not reality. We will discuss the success rates of timing the market and actively trading later in this section. For now, just know that it is extremely rare for anyone, professional or not, to consistently beat the market. It is even rarer for a professional to beat the market by more than what it costs to hire them—beating the market by 0.5% and charging you 1% ultimately results in a 0.5% opportunity cost on your end.

How to Get Started

You will first need to open a brokerage account. A brokerage account is a portal that allows you to buy and sell securities and Exchange-Traded Funds (ETFs). There are many companies that offer great features for the end user, and after setting up your account, using the system to purchase

Beware: Whole Life Insurance

Beware of insurance salesmen who present themselves as financial advisers. Whole life insurance is a policy that you carry for your entire life as opposed to a term life insurance, which is almost always the better option for most people. There are some benefits to whole life insurance, which mainly include the following: Your cash value increases (though not nearly as quickly as traditional investments), you could be paid dividends for holding the policy, and there are also some tax benefits for beneficiaries. However, the death benefit is tiny compared to the death benefit provided by term life insurance, sometimes as much as 10× smaller for the same premium. Note that whole life insurance is a form of permanent life insurance. Other forms of permanent life insurance include Indexed Universal Life (IUL) and Universal Life.

Most importantly, whole life insurance is commonly sold by insurance salespeople, who make massive commissions when you sign up. If you cancel the policy, you only get a small fraction of what you put into it as a "surrender amount." The major issue with whole life policies isn't necessarily the policy itself; it is that the insurance salespeople often operate under the guise of financial advisers. Many people have had friends and family offer to "manage their finances" for them but ultimately sell them insurance. There are a specific group of people who may benefit from such a policy, but unless you are mega rich, you are better off spending money on a term life insurance policy and investing the difference in cost. An insurance company will not have your financial interests at heart. Their only job is to sell insurance and make a commission. If you need an unbiased financial plan, read a book like this or find a fee-only fiduciary CFP to help you with your investment portfolio. If your "financial adviser" starts to tell you about whole life insurance, it is guaranteed that they are an insurance salesperson.

investments is just as easy as buying stuff on Amazon. The most popular brokerages are:

- Vanguard
- Fidelity

- Charles Schwab
- E-Trade

The brokerage account can be any type of account (see the *Types of Investment Accounts* section). You are allowed to open multiple different types of accounts under the same brokerage. Once you open your account, you will need to fund money into the account by linking your checking account. Be aware of the annual contribution limits on certain account types.

Once you have money in your account, you are ready to put your money to work! If this makes you nervous, then I have good news for you! You can set your cash funding and security purchasing to be automatic on a monthly basis. The act of investing the same amount from month to month is called dollar cost averaging (DCA), and it is a great way to help you consistently invest while reducing the psychological burden of investing everything all at once and watching it go up and down. Each platform will have slightly different user experiences, so be sure to read through how to set that up on each platform.

You can trade stocks, mutual funds, and index funds with $0 cost per trade in most brokerage firms today. You specify the security that you want to purchase via its ticker symbol and then select the number of shares you wish to buy or sell. A ticker symbol is a code for a company that helps identify the company (e.g., Apple is AAPL; AT&T is T; S&P 500 ETF by Vanguard is VOO; etc.).

Once you purchase those shares, they will show up in your assets along with your cash balance. The simplest method is to use the "market purchase" option, which purchases the shares at whatever price the shares are the moment you click the "buy" button. I don't need to set any fancy limit orders, which wait until the stock hits a certain price until it executes the trade. The money saved by getting the shares $0.20 cheaper is inconsequential. The act of committing the cash to an investment is orders of magnitude more meaningful than saving a fraction of a dollar on each share while risking not getting the shares at all due to the limit price not being met.

What Can I Invest In?

Stocks Versus Bonds

While there are a myriad of different asset types, there are two main assets that will have a spot in your portfolio: stocks and bonds. They are fundamentally different and backed by different assets.

Stocks are shares of a company that you are able to purchase. For example, if Scott Gong Tutoring (SGT) were to need capital, I might turn to the students of Virginia Tech and say that we are looking for investors for our company. There are 100 shares of SGT available, each providing 1% ownership of the company. The initial stated valuation of SGT is $500,000 (I can dream right?), which means each share is going to sell for $5,000. If people agree with the valuation, they will purchase shares. I then take the capital acquired and pursue capital ventures—I use that money to make more money. If my company begins to profit, then I might return some of that money to my shareholders in the form of dividends. Let's say I return $250 to my shareholders as a thank-you for holding the stock. Other people might see this and say, "I want to buy SGT shares too! Hey, I will buy your shares for $5,100." This continues as the value generated from SGT and public perception of the company change over time. While this example is vastly simplified, millions of comparable transactions occur daily in real time on the New York Stock Exchange (NYSE).

As you might imagine, stocks can be pretty risky too! If SGT fails to provide a reputable tutoring service, its investors might lose confidence and sell their shares to avoid further losses, causing the share price to go down. In general, short-term fluctuations in the share price of a company are largely due to speculation while the long-term price trend is more rooted in the performance of the company in the marketplace.

Minimizing short-term fluctuations due to individual stocks requires diversification—spreading your eggs in multiple baskets and, in this case, companies. How many companies do you need to be diversified? 10? 100? 1,000? Generally speaking, to be properly diversified, you not only need many different companies, but the companies that you invest in must also be diversified. For example, Coca Cola owns dozens of other companies and is a highly diversified individual company while Snapchat is not. As a rule of thumb, you want no more than 5% of your portfolio in a single company, which means that 20 companies is the minimum amount for proper diversification. You may think it might be challenging to buy and manage so many stocks at once. Enter the index fund—which is covered in detail in the next section.

Bonds: While stocks are intrinsically valued on the company from which they are issued, bonds are backed by an entity. When you purchase a stock, you are purchasing a part of a company. When you purchase a bond, you are loaning the entity some amount of money that is to be repaid with a predetermined amount of interest after a certain period of time. For example, you can purchase a 20-year U.S. Treasury Bond that returns 3.875% at the time of writing. You must keep this bond for 20 years, and you will be guaranteed the return of 3.875% as long as the government still exists in 20 years. The downside to this is that you must keep this bond for 20 years or pay penalties if terminated before maturity.

Fortunately, when people recommend investing in bonds, they don't mean buying physical bonds; rather, it means investing in the bond market. Much like the shares of a company, people are able to buy and sell bonds as the government interest rates rise and fall compared to the fixed interest rate of the bond. This all happens in the bond market. For the purposes of this book, all discussions about allocating money to bonds mean purchasing bonds in index/mutual fund form (BND/VBTLX). These are funds composed of bond offerings from many different companies and reduces the complexity as well as the risk that any individual company will not be able to pay you back. Additionally, it allows vastly more liquidity than purchasing a 20-year Treasury bond from the U.S. government.

Key Takeaways: Stocks are parts of companies. A collection of stocks can be purchased in the form of an index fund. Bonds are loans that we give to companies in return for a percentage back. Bonds can be bought and sold like stocks and can be purchased in the form of index funds as well.

Mutual Funds Versus ETFs Versus Index Funds

You have seen the abovementioned terms used many times in this book already, and they will continue to be used. However, it is important to note that these terms, while similar, are not always interchangeable. Let's go over the definitions of each and discuss the subtle differences:

- Mutual Funds are managed (either actively or passively) by a money management professional. They can consist of stocks and other types of assets. Mutual fund trades are executed only once at the end of the day. They also generally have higher fees than other types of funds and can have a minimum investment amount.
- Exchange-Traded Funds are collections of stocks that can be traded like a regular stock. Generally, they are not managed but can be. They require no minimum investment and fees are generally low.
- Index Funds track a specific index of stocks, such as the S&P 500. Both mutual funds and ETFs can track indexes. For example, Vanguard has both mutual fund and ETF versions of their "total stock market" fund (VTSAX and VTI). They have slightly different expense ratios but ultimately track the same index. When referring to an "index fund," it is important to remember that some index funds may be mutual funds and some may be ETFs. There is an index for everything. In fact, there are more index funds in the United States than there are individual companies. You can find an index fund for tech, green energy, oil, commodities, precious metals, and even crypto. Note that being defined as an index fund doesn't automatically reduce risk or provide ample diversification. It is important to understand the holdings of each index fund before purchasing it.

If all of this terminology makes your head spin, don't worry. The differences between them will have minimal impact on your investment strategy as long as you invest in funds that have low fees and you understand what they invest in.

What Should I Invest In?

In general, the best hands-off asset that you can purchase is a low-cost, properly diversified, broad market index fund. A properly diversified index fund contains a lot of companies so that you are not directly subjected to the volatility of any single company.

Let's discuss some of the most popular index funds out there and their compositions. For simplicity, we will use Vanguard's funds, but Fidelity and other brokerages have their own versions as well. One is not better than the other, and it comes down to preference. This list is in building block order:

- VOO: S&P 500 index fund (500 biggest and most successful companies in the United States)
- VTI: 84% VOO/16% Small–midcap[25] stocks (has almost every public stock in the United States)
- VXUS: 100% international fund (no U.S. stocks)
- VT: 62% VTI / 38% VXUS (blend of U.S. total market and international)
- VTSAX: Mutual fund version of VTI index fund ($3,000 minimum investment)
- BNDX: Total International Bond ETF
- BND: Total Bond Market ETF

Note that the terms small-cap, midcap, and so on have to do with the size of the market cap of the company.

If you don't care about all of that stuff you can simply VTI (or VTSAX) and chill. A portfolio consisting of 100% VTI is plenty of diversification for a young professional. Your question now is likely this: Why no international or bond exposure? Let's look at the reasons you *might* consider omitting each from your portfolio:

International Exposure: VTI is composed mostly of the 500 largest companies in the United States (VTI has 8,500+ holdings, but most of the weight is in the top 500 companies). Most of those 500 companies operate internationally. Therefore, there is a fair bit of international exposure through induction. There is an extra layer of complexity with international investments: the currency exchange rate. Changing exchange rates add a layer of risk that makes international investments potentially riskier than rewarding. Many financial experts recommend having a 10% allocation to international funds simply to have that exposure in the event that the United States is outperformed by other markets. You can always start out with 100% U.S. stocks and then add international as you hone your investing strategy. If you want 10% international exposure off the bat, you can simply purchase 3 parts VTI (0% international) and 1 part VT (about 37% international) or 9 parts VTI and 1 part VXUS.

Bond Exposure: Bonds are an excellent way to smooth out the ups and downs of your stock portfolio since they are more stable. However, what you gain in stability you lose in potential growth—the classic trade-off between growth and risk. Studies show that a small bond exposure in your portfolio (about 10%) actually outperforms a 100% stock portfolio, but does so only in specific ranges of time, namely when the market is bearish—trending downward. Therefore, most young investors find it beneficial to leave bonds out of their portfolio until they are about a decade or two out from retirement. Keep in mind that swings in your investment portfolio don't matter if you aren't planning on withdrawing the money anytime soon.

To summarize, don't be afraid if your investment strategy is basic. Investing does not need to be complicated. If you invest in a low-cost, highly diversified, broad market index fund, you will outperform most Wall Street fund managers and their fees in the long run.

Honorable Mention: John (Jack) Bogle (1929–2019) was the father of the modern index fund and founder of the Vanguard Group. He was a champion of low-cost and broadly diversified index funds, which reduce risk through diversification and reduce costs by being passively managed versus actively managed like mutual funds. Investing is a zero-sum game, which means that for every winner, there is a loser. After you factor in costs, it becomes a negative sum game.

Broad market and highly diversified index funds > actively managed mutual funds

This is true for many reasons:

- Actively managed mutual funds cost money to manage— people do research on expensive computers, work in offices with high operating costs, and investors get paid a lot of money to trade.

- Actively managed mutual funds are tax inefficient—whenever stocks are bought and sold, they are subject to capital gains taxes. Actively managed portfolios are rebalanced regularly in hopes of beating the market.
- Only a small percentage of mutual funds outperform the market in the long run, and this is skewed even further by the survivorship bias—most of those that lose money aren't around anymore.

Picking Stocks

No matter how much you love index funds, there might be a speckle of hope in the back of your mind that you could buy and hold a group of stocks that will outperform the S&P 500 or Total Market Index. Although the odds of doing so are extremely small, it is not impossible. In general, the stocks you should consider adding to your portfolio should not exceed about 5% of your overall portfolio. When selecting stocks to invest in, choose companies you understand well and feel confident investing in. Don't follow investing advice online if you don't understand the fundamentals. You should be able to describe what this company does to make money, how this company operates, how its balance sheet compares to its competitors, what differentiates this company from its competitors, and why the company is timeless (i.e., why it would be considered a good long-term investment) to a 5-year-old. That is the litmus test that you should use to determine whether you understand how a company works. Warren Buffet is frequently regarded as one of the greatest investors of all time. He was one of the people, along with Ben Graham and Charlie Munger, who popularized value investing—purchasing undervalued stocks that you understand the basis of and holding them forever. You can choose your own stocks so long as it isn't a huge portion of your portfolio. If you do, keep in mind one quote from Warren Buffet: "Only buy something that you'd be perfectly happy to hold if the market shut down for 10 years."

Dividends

A *dividend* is a cash payout from a stock or index fund that you receive as a reward for holding the stock! No, it's not a scam. In reality, what you've done upon purchasing shares of a company is invested in that company and provided them with capital to seek profits through their business. Upon receiving profits, they pay a portion to their shareholders and keep a portion for themselves to reinvest in the business. There are many details about dividends that we will not address at length in this book, but the essence of dividends is that they are portions of a company's profits that are paid on a monthly or quarterly basis to the shareholders in cash. You can find the dividend amount, if there is one, under the "Dividend and Yield" box in the stock info. Your dividend is typically taxable as normal income unless you are in a tax-deferred account or are receiving *qualified dividends*, which are fully or partially tax-exempt per the IRS.

Because of compound interest, you may realize that the best use of dividend money early in your investing career is to reinvest it back into your portfolio. Generally speaking, this is the best course of action. In retirement, you might keep your dividends as income.

Suppose VTI pays a $0.82 dividend per share each quarter. Even if you have 100 shares (valued at about $200/share as of April 2023 for a $20,000 position), you still won't have enough to purchase an entire share of VTI with each dividend payout. Only select brokerage accounts allow the purchase of fractional shares, but that is improving for the better. On top of that, if you receive dividends from multiple investments, it may be challenging and time-consuming to decide where to reinvest them. Enter the dividend reinvestment plan (DRIP), a tool to help you reinvest dividends without thinking about it.

DRIP is a setting you can toggle on or off for any particular investment and tells your brokerage to automatically reinvest the dividend from a particular investment directly back into that investment in the form of fractional shares. The extra kick from reinvesting the dividend, although seemingly small today, will result in a huge addition to your future earnings.

Beware: Annuities

An annuity is an asset that you purchase with a lump sum of cash that pays you over a set period of time. Most often, annuities are products you purchase from insurance companies. You can probably imagine where I am going with this—there are huge commissions associated with selling an annuity as an insurance company! The upside to an annuity is that it offers a stable and guaranteed source of income for a set price. The downside is, again, extremely high fees. There are several types of annuities, which are differentiated by the method in which they are funded (lump sum or periodic), when you take the payments (immediately or after some time), and how long you will receive payments (for a certain number of years or until death). Essentially, while life insurance is protection against not living long enough, annuities are protection against living too long and running out of money. The bottom line is that like whole life insurance, annuities are often sold as investments when they are actually forms of insurance. Annuities are suitable for a very small percentage of the population, and it is important to know when you are that person and when you are not. In general, anything that is sold to you by a salesman will be financially inefficient—look up the average annual compensation of insurance or annuity salesmen and you will understand why.

Risk, Reward, and Liquidity

Everyone has heard of the risk versus reward trade-off. In general, riskier investments tend to have a higher return *potential*, and safer investments tend to have lower return *potential*. Notice the use of the word "potential." This is in general. If investments are too risky and don't return enough, they are simply poor investments. If you find investments that seem really safe and have unusually high returns, then it may be too good to be true. Investments that have high returns with relatively low risks exist, but they usually require lots of personal commitment of either time or expertise, which can be major downsides on a larger scale. In other words, they rely on your time or expertise to reduce or manage risk. It is your job to understand your personal risk tolerance and select your balance of investments accordingly.

In addition to risk versus reward, there is reward versus liquidity. Liquidity is how quickly you can convert an asset into cash. There is *qualitative* value in having relatively quick access to your assets. The *quantitative* value is up to you to decide. For example, you are debating whether you should place your money into a HYSA that currently pays an after-tax rate of 3.5% or pay off your mortgage that has an interest rate of 4%. While, mathematically, paying off the mortgage will yield you a higher rate of return, you have virtually zero liquidity in that option, which means the money you pay into your mortgage is inaccessible unless you refinance (which costs money), sell the home (also costs money), or use a Home Equity Line of Credit or Home Equity Loan (both of which have cost money and have higher interest rates than your mortgage). On the other hand, you can have cash in hand from a HYSA within a few hours or days depending on your bank. The cost of keeping cash in your savings account is technically 0.5%, but to some that is a small price to pay for liquidity! In this specific instance, one might choose to purchase treasury bonds or CDs, which lock up money for a shorter duration like 1 to 5 years and pay slightly higher interest rates than the HYSA.

Time in the Market > Timing the Market

You may feel that you can outsmart the market by buying low and selling high. While that does sound great in theory, the reality is that VERY few people are able to beat a broad market index fund in long-term performance. You will constantly hear stories about people who made $69k by trading Tesla or people who were able to retire by buying Dogecoin crypto. What those folks will never tell you is how much money they lose in the market in order to generate these wins or how long they've been winning for. People who win that big rarely stop there. They increase the stakes until they inevitably invest a huge amount in a losing stock. Warren Buffett, often regarded as the most successful investor of all time, once famously bet hedge funds $1M that they couldn't beat the S&P 500 over the next 10 years. Hedge fund managers, using some of the best tools, working with some of the smartest Wall Street investors on the planet, were unable to beat a broad market index fund over 10 years[26]. To add a cherry on top, this bet started *before* the 2008 crash. Buffett held onto a broad market index fund through the 2008 crash, didn't buy or sell a single share of it, and outperformed a group of the best investors in the world who were actively trading for 10 years straight. Legendary.

The moral of this story is to focus on getting into the market early and consistently rather than finding the best time to get in all at once. This concept of time in the market beating timing the market is critical. Consider the following (Table 8.1):

Table 8.1 Best versus worst timing of market versus DCA

$2,000 invested into the S&P 500 every year from 2000 to 2020 This would be $40,000 total invested over 20 years. The ending results are as follows:		
Scenario	**Ending amount**	**Average return**
Holding U.S. Treasury Bills	$44,438	1.1%
Buying at the lowest point of each year (perfect timing)	$151,391	12.4%
Buying at the highest point of each year (worst timing)	$121,171	10.5%
Buying immediately on the first trading day in January	$135,471	11.5%
DCA on the first trading day of each month	$134,856	11.4%

Keep in mind that this is investing through both the tech bubble of the early 2000s and the housing market crash of 2008. We can immediately see that while there is a difference between the best and worst timing of the market, nobody in history has been able to time every market high or low for 20 years straight. Note that even the Worst Timing scenario still netted over 10% annual gains for the entire period. Your best bet will be to get in the market as early as possible and not wait. Consider Scenario 4 versus Scenario 5. Splitting your annual investment into small chunks and investing a chunk each month seems like a better strategy than throwing it all in on January 1st, but since the market goes up more often than it goes down, this is statistically inefficient. However, if it helps you psychologically, then go right ahead. Historically you'll be giving up 0.1% in annual growth, but if it helps you sleep better at night then the sacrifice is worth it.

You may think you might be purchasing stocks right before a big crash, but people have been talking about the next big crash every single year since the last big crash. Michael Burry, the man who predicted the 2008 crash, has been regularly announcing the next big crash since 2008. He's been wrong every time thus far. You also may fear that you are purchasing stocks at an all-time high. If the market goes up, then technically it will always be at an all-time high. Every historical all-time high has been eclipsed by a new all-time high! In fact, several highs have been eclipsed during the writing of this book. The beauty of compound growth is that if you zoom out on a multi-decade chart, these "big crashes" are blips in the continuously upward trend that you will hopefully ride out regardless of short-term market conditions. Here is the "time to recover" from various financial crisis of the last 30 years if you bought lump sum at the very top immediately before it crashed:

- 2000 tech bubble: 7 years (August 2000–October 2007)
- 2008 Great Recession: 5.5 years (October 2007–March 2013)
- COVID-19 crash: 7 months (January 2020–July 2020)

Let's look at the zoomed-out view of the S&P 500 since 1928. Statistically speaking, it is more worthwhile simply to invest without timing versus trying to catch the dips in the chart of which, as you can see, there are few (Figure 8.1).

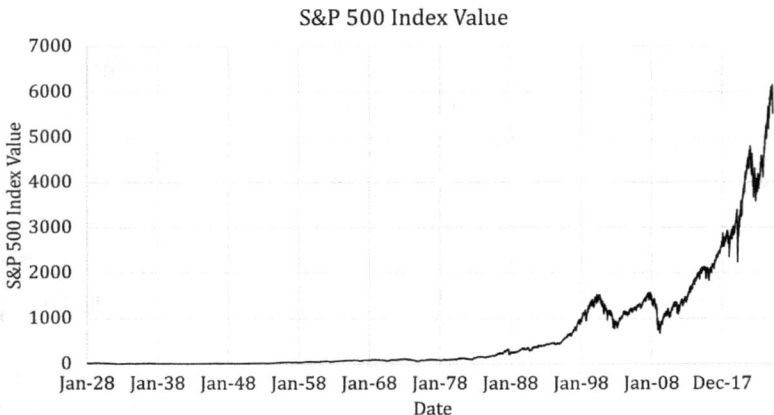

Figure 8.1 S&P 500 index value

Again, nobody in the history of mankind has properly timed the bottom or top of each market year for 20 years in a row. Nobody. The difference between picking the top and picking the bottom of each year is, for all intents and purposes, negligible. In fact, the blips in the market are excellent opportunities to buy at a discount. The stock market is the only store that people leave when things are on sale!

Annualizing the S&P 500 chart into yearly returns yields the following chart, which demonstrates the frequency in which the index ends higher than it started in any given year (Figure 8.2).

S&P 500 Annual Growth Since 1928

Figure 8.2 S&P 500 annual growth since 1928

The last relevant concept to debunking market timing is the efficient market hypothesis (EMH), which states that stocks are always trading at their true market value since information about the stock is instantly available to everyone. It is therefore nearly impossible to regularly pick undervalued stocks or predict trends via technical analysis. The theory states that if you receive information that might make you believe a stock has a certain value or will trade a certain way, it means that everybody in the market has also received that information at approximately the same time as you, and the effect of that information has already been priced into the value of the stock.

In the famous words of Warren Buffett:

I could improve your ultimate financial welfare by giving you a ticket with only 20 slots in it so that you had 20 punches—representing all the investments that you got to make in a lifetime. And once you'd punched through the card, you couldn't make any more investments at all. Under those rules, you'd really think carefully about what you did and you'd be forced to load up on what you'd really thought about. So you'd do so much better.

The idea is to think really hard about any decision in order to make the right choice. Ideally, you want to do as little as possible and keep it simple. You do not need to go in and out of the stock market in order to make money. Buffett's philosophy is not to choose 20 stocks that will win but, rather, to make your decisions wisely. A "decision" does not have to be an investment in a particular company. A decision might be to auto-invest 20% of your income each year into fund XYZ and not touch it until retirement. Excellent! Punch a hole in the card and check back in 30 years. Five years later you might choose to purchase an investment property in an area that you know well and either learn how to manage an investment property or hire a good manager. Great! Punch another two holes in your card. Seventeen decisions to go. Additionally, Buffett emphasizes that you don't even need 20 "wins" to get rich—you only need a handful. Buffett has made numerous investments over the decades. Most are not memorable and some even lost money. His big winners are the ones that made him truly rich, for example, investing in Apple in the 2000s.

Ultimately, the point of this section is that you cannot time the market and you will be playing a fool's game if you continuously try to beat the market. To round out this section, let us appreciate a quote: "The best time to plant a tree was 20 years ago, the next best time is now."

Investment Tools That Make Life Easy

If you have no interest in managing your own portfolio the traditional way, I have good news for you! There are plenty of options that allow you to be almost completely hands-off with your investments once you set them up.

Robo-Investors

Robo-Investors are a great way to get investing without going through the complicated setup and self-management. Essentially, a robo-manager is a computer-managed brokerage account that maintains a certain balance in a portfolio using a preset algorithm. The portfolio balance is based on information that you input into the system, such as your risk tolerance and desired retirement date. Typically, the fees are much lower than a traditional financial adviser and require less effort than doing it yourself. A popular robo-investment platform is Acorns,[27] which originally started off as a way of investing spare change. It costs $3/month (free for a few years with a .edu e-mail) and is a fantastic "set it and forget it" investment. Other popular robo-investor platforms are Betterment, SoFi Automated Investing, Wealthfront, and Vanguard Digital Advisor. There are many options out there, and they're typically low cost (between 0% and 0.3% of total portfolio value).

Your robo-investors are brokerages that automatically invest the money that you give them and will invest based on either the risk profile you select or the asset allocation you predetermine. They may also automatically implement tax loss harvesting strategies. For example, you place $100 per week into a brokerage account. You want 90% of it allocated toward stocks, and 10% toward bonds. Instead of having to calculate how many shares of each asset you need to purchase, the robo-investor does it for you and automatically purchases them! Then, let's say that your stocks go down and your bonds go up. You are no longer at 90/10 split, more like 89/11 split. Your robo-investor will then allocate more of your new deposits toward stocks to help you get back to the 90/10 split. It requires no effort on your part aside from looking at it every so often, and even that is optional.

The case for robo-advisers is that they help folks who are afraid of investing begin to invest with a smaller amount of personal involvement. The case against them is that if you solely use a robo-adviser, you will not learn the ins and outs of investing. While having an algorithm manage $5,000 for you today might not seem like a big deal, what if it's managing $50,000 or $500,000 or $5,000,000? When would you want to make the switch and learn how to manage yourself? Would you be comfortable managing $500,000 on your own for the first time with no investing experience? This isn't to say that robo-investors aren't good for people with large investments; rather, you should understand how they fit into the big picture of your portfolio.

Target Date Funds

If everything you've read so far about investing and asset allocation is going way over your head, you may be tempted to hire a financial adviser to take care of it for you. However, there is yet another option that is low cost and requires virtually zero effort on your end apart from setting up the account and the direct deposit (pay yourself first, remember?). Enter the target date fund (TDF).

TDFs are another great way that offer a slightly different level of autonomy. Recall that at the most basic level, your investment portfolio should consist of some split of stocks and bonds. Let's say you decide on a 90/10 stock/bond split. As you near retirement, you would want to increase your bond allocation to reduce risk. You may want to target 70/30 within 5 years of retirement and then 60/40 during retirement. Because stocks and bonds don't necessarily rise and fall together, it is mathematically arduous to get the allocations perfect! Your TDF will automatically redistribute your investments as you near the retirement year of choice. For example, if I choose a Vanguard TDF VTTSX, the Target Retirement 2060 Fund, it will automatically allocate accordingly so that I would be properly allocated in stocks and bonds in the year 2060, when I plan on retiring. Keep in mind that a TDF is a Mutual Fund and not an Index Fund, which means that it is actively managed rather than passively managed. Therefore, the expense ratios may be slightly higher. However, don't let this deter you from using them if that is what you need to use in order to invest consistently. TDFs are a very powerful way to achieve your goals with minimal effort and are a great asset to hold in an account that is not as easily accessible or manageable, such as a company-sponsored 401(k). Many company-sponsored 401(k) plans are notoriously challenging to self-manage. The TDF is a great choice for such accounts.

Types of Investment Accounts

You can typically segregate your investment accounts by the tax advantage offered, if applicable. As mentioned in the tax section, "Nothing is certain except death and taxes"—Ben Franklin. In this section, we will discuss some ways to reduce your tax liability in your working years and retirement years. The government and IRS offer many ways to shield your hard-earned money from taxes as long as you know the rules.

You are taxed everywhere in life. Let's say that you own a shop that sells t-shirts. You sell a $20 shirt; the customer pays 5% sales tax ($1).

You earn a $10 profit on that shirt, so you have to pay 25% income tax on your profits ($2.50). When you take the remaining $7.50 and invest it into your regular brokerage account, you make $5 profit. Of that $5 you have to pay 10% capital gains taxes on it ($0.50). When you take that $12.00 out of your account and go purchase a burger and fries, you are also taxed at 5% sales tax ($0.60)—and the cycle repeats.

The numbers are simply approximations, but the gist is there: You are taxed on everything. Luckily, there are some ways to avoid one or more of the taxes by using special accounts that the government has provided to reduce tax burden, even though there are limitations and rules surrounding their application.

Pretax Versus Roth Versus Taxable

In this section, we will discuss the meaning of the different tax advantages of various accounts. These tax advantages are distinctions and not necessarily "types" of accounts, but rather different forms of tax benefits (or lack thereof). You can open each of these types of accounts with any brokerage company.

- Taxable accounts are accounts where there is no tax advantage. You must pay income tax on the money placed into the account, taxes on dividends received while you are holding the securities, and capital gains taxes on your profit when you sell your securities. Although there are typically IRS-set limits for tax-advantaged, there is no limit on taxable investment accounts, which is why they are a great tool for high earners.
  - Pros: Money can be placed in and withdrawn at any time in any amount. Long-term investments are taxed in a lower tax system than even pretax retirement accounts, which are taxed as ordinary income.
  - Cons: You are taxed three times (once going in, once coming out, and on your dividends).
- Pretax accounts (i.e., traditional accounts) are accounts in which the money placed into the account is pretax, meaning that you

do not pay federal taxes on money going into that account. Note that FICA taxes still need to be paid on money going in, but not on withdrawals. In other words, this can be considered a "deduction" on your federal tax filing. Typically, traditional accounts start as pretax and are taxed as regular income (sans FICA tax) upon withdrawal. You also don't pay taxes on dividends received in this account.

- ○ Pros: You save money up front at your marginal tax rate, which allows a greater amount of money to grow tax free.
- ○ Cons: You have to pay taxes when you sell, and you are unsure about what the tax rate and your income will be when you sell. Money typically has to stay in until retirement age or taken out using alternative methods.

- Roth accounts are accounts in which you pay tax on the invested money upfront, but your money grows tax free. This means that upon withdrawal, you will take home 100% of the money in your account.
  - ○ Pros: No capital gains tax, which means future increases in taxes will have no effect on your investment. No taxes on dividends. Contributions can be withdrawn penalty-free after *seasoning period*, if applicable. Easy to transfer to heirs due to taxes being paid already.
  - ○ Cons: Most people pay more taxes prior to retirement than they do in retirement, which makes the tax benefit of Roth less helpful than a Pretax benefit.

A savvy investor has a combination of all three of these accounts in their portfolios. The reason is that there are two main variables between today and your retirement: your income and the tax rates. Well, technically it's three things: income, expenses, and tax rates. However, in retirement your income should equal your expenses as you will only withdraw what you need from your investment accounts. The exception to this is if you are subject to required minimum distributions (RMDs[28]), which is the government's way of forcing you to withdraw money from a pretax account to subsequently pay taxes.

The Independent Retirement Arrangement (IRA)

An IRA is a tax-advantaged account that you can open through any of the brokerage companies mentioned earlier. It is self-managed and, depending on the specific account type, has some limitations.

Contributions to a traditional (or pretax) IRA can only be deducted if you do not have a company-sponsored 401(k) and make below the annual income limit of $79k/year. Note that anyone can contribute to a traditional IRA, but only the people who meet the income criteria can take the tax deduction.

Since contributions to the Roth IRA are nondeductible, the only limitation is your income. Eligibility begins phasing out at $150k for 2025. When your MAGI reaches $165k, you are ineligible to contribute to a Roth IRA. Because contributed funds are post-tax, you can withdraw contributed funds at any time, granted your account is over 5 years old.

The annual contribution for both types of IRAs is $7,000/year for tax year 2025. Note that there are penalties for contributing more than you are allowed, typically 6% for every year that the excess contribution stays in the account. If you are unsure of whether your income will exceed the Roth IRA income limit, use the backdoor Roth method. The contribution window is January 1st of the contribution year until April 15th (tax day) of the following year.

Backdoor Roth IRA

The Roth IRA has an income limit of $150k/year at which your allowable contribution begins to phase out and is capped at $165k/year, after which you'll not be able to contribute at all. For simplicity, we'll focus on the $150k/year to allow the full deposit amount. Note that this is the MAGI, which is your income after your 401(k) (or other pretax) contributions and other deductions like health insurance. The pretax IRA has an income limit of $79k/year. If you are above this amount, you are ineligible to *deduct* the contribution from your taxes, but you are still allowed to make an after-tax, or *nondeductible*, contribution to the account.

Since there is no income limit for after-tax contributions to your pretax IRA, you can contribute to your pretax IRA, then perform a Roth conversion on your cash. This allows you to legally get around the Roth IRA income limit!

Note that typically you are subject to income tax when rolling a Pretax account into a Roth account, but since you do this in the same tax year, you will simply not take the deduction on your taxes (you won't be allowed to anyways), and you will not be subject to additional tax versus contributing directly to your Roth IRA. Another way to think about it is that you are making a taxed contribution to a pretax account and using the pretax account as a vehicle to move money into your Roth account through the "back door."

The downsides of the backdoor method are that you must account for the "seasoning period" and Pro-Rata Rule. Recall that funds contributed to the Roth IRA can be withdrawn at any time penalty-free granted that your account is more than 5 years old. The seasoning period states that all funds rolled over or converted[29] into your Roth IRA must be kept in the account for at least 5 years before withdrawal. Therefore, you must plan 5 years ahead when attempting to access pretax funds to avoid fees. This is only applicable if you plan on retiring early since withdrawals after 59 and half years old are penalty free.

Then, the Pro-Rata rule comes into effect when your pretax account contains actual pretax contributions. Recall that in a pure backdoor Roth setting, your pretax account is simply a medium of transfer for your post-tax money to reach the Roth IRA. However, it's possible that you have rolled over funds from a 401(k) from a previous employer. Those funds are pretax. If you contribute after-tax funds to your Pretax IRA, you will trigger the Pro-Rata rule in your rollover. This rule states that if you initiate a rollover from your Pretax IRA to a Roth IRA, you must pay taxes on the percentage of funds that are pretax.

Suppose you have $63,000 in your Pretax IRA that was rolled over from a previous job's 401(k). You use the backdoor method to contribute $7,000 to your IRA with the intention of rolling over that $7,000 to your Roth IRA. Your total account balance is $70,000, but 90% of your account balance is pretax. When you roll over your $7,000 to your Roth IRA, your brokerage will grab $6,300 from your pretax bucket and $700 from your after-tax bucket. Therefore, you will be required to pay taxes on $6,300. Note that you are unable to escape the Pro-Rata rule even if you use separate accounts for your 401(k) rollover and your backdoor Roth.

The bottom line for Backdoor Roth IRA is that if you anticipate exceeding the income limit for the standard Roth IRA, you should take the following steps:

1. Contribute the desired amount to your Pretax IRA and wait for the money to clear—this typically takes a few business days.
2. Go into your Pretax IRA and initiate a Roth conversion.
3. Once the money clears to your Roth IRA, you can invest as usual.
4. You may need to withhold taxes from the Pro-Rata Rule.
5. Remember to file IRS form 8606 for Nondeductible IRAs.

As with many finance things, there is indeed a way around the Pro-Rata rule. Instead of rolling your 401(k) from your previous employer over to your Pretax IRA, you *might* be able to roll it over into your new employer's 401(k), thereby avoiding the space in which a Roth conversion might take place. Check to see if your new employer's 401(k) plan allows for this.

Mega-Backdoor Roth IRA

While the Backdoor Roth IRA is a fairly well-known method among high earners, the Mega-backdoor Roth[30] is not since it is only available through certain employers. The logic is as follows:

1. You can only contribute $23,500/year to your 401(k) per the 2025 IRS limit.
2. Your company allows you to contribute up to 30% of your $100k paycheck (some companies do not have a restriction).
3. Your total annual contribution is $30k, but only $23.5k of it can go into your Pretax 401(k).
4. After the IRS limit is fulfilled some three-fourths of the way through the year, the last $6.5k of your contribution goes into a regular taxable account that is still managed by your company's financial provider.

5. At the end of the year, you can roll the $6.5k taxable account balance from your employer's financial provider into your own Roth IRA. There are no restrictions on this since you have not taken any deductions, and rollovers have no annual limits.

6. You have now added an additional $6.5k to your annual tax-advantaged accounts. Note that this does not affect your regular Roth IRA contribution since it is considered a rollover and not a contribution.

7. Notes about the MBDR:

    a. Your annual contribution is limited by the percentage of your income your employer allows you to contribute or the IRS total contribution limit of $70,000.

    b. You need to make sure that the financial management company your company uses allows you to roll over the money into your IRA. Some companies only allow you to initiate such a rollover when you leave the company.

    c. You need to ensure that your company will continue to provide their % match after you've hit your annual contribution limit for your 401(k).

Other Tax-Advantaged Accounts

- Health Savings Account (HSA): The HSA is the only tax-advantaged account that is triple-tax-advantaged. The contributions are investable and tax deductible. The growth (i.e., dividends) and the withdrawals are tax free. This makes it an incredible vehicle for savings, particularly for the inevitable health expenses later in life. The drawback is that withdrawals can only be used to reimburse qualified health expenses, hence the name. The trick is that you do not need to reimburse yourself immediately. As long as you keep the receipt, you can reimburse yourself at any time in the future. Note that you must have a high-deductible health plan (HDHP) to be eligible for an HSA. For 2025, the annual contribution limit for self-only coverage is $4,300 (or $8,550 for your entire family). You can make non-qualified withdrawals from your HSA for a 20% penalty on top of the withdrawal being taxed as ordinary income.

- Flexible Savings Account (FSA): The FSA is used to keep pretax money that can be used for qualified medical expenses.[31] However, this account is not investable and is simply cash that is deducted from your paycheck. Contributions can only be made via payroll deduction. The annual limit for the FSA is comparable to the HSA at $3,300 annually for 2025, but the drawback is that only $660 can be carried over from year to year. If you don't use it by December 31st, it's gone. Luckily, there are a myriad of items that are FSA eligible, including over-the-counter medication, first aid kits, feminine hygiene products, doctor copays, and more!
- Simplified Employee Pension IRA (SEP IRA)[32]: This account is a pretax IRA for folks who are self-employed and have employees. The contribution limit is the lesser of 25% of net income or $70k/year in 2025. Like a normal 401(k), both the employer and employee can contribute to the account. Note that as long as your business is registered properly and you follow the contribution limits, you are eligible to contribute to this account in addition to a company-sponsored 401(k) and a Roth IRA, although the TOTAL contribution limit for pretax accounts of this type (not Roth IRA) is limited by the IRS to $23.5k/year in 2025.
- Solo 401(k)[33]: This account is similar to the SEP IRA but intended for use with a single participant; that is, your company has no employees. In the solo 401(k), the sole owner acts as both the employee and the employer, and is therefore allowed to contribute up to $70k/year of earned income, not including catch-up contributions. Like a SEP IRA, you are eligible to have a solo 401(k) in addition to a company-sponsored 401(k) if you follow the contribution limits ($23.5k in 2025). The TOTAL contribution to your company-sponsored 401(k) and your Solo 401(k) cannot exceed the maximum amount in any given year.
- 529 (Education Account): This is a Roth-type account that you can use to save for educational expenses. Most people use the 529 to save for their children's college expenses, but you can also use it to further your own education! Capital gains are not taxed, and there is no annual contribution limit (although you are subject to gift tax if you exceed the annual *reporting* limit). The catch is that

you are only allowed to use this money for education expenses; otherwise, there is a penalty. However, a law that went into effect in 2024 will allow up to $35,000 of leftover funds in a 529 to be rolled over into a Roth IRA, granted that the 529 account is more than 15 years old. Note that the rollover counts toward the annual Roth IRA limit while other rollovers do not.

The 401(k)

A 401(k) is a company-sponsored investment account that is managed by a financial institution of your employer's choosing. Traditionally, the 401(k) is a pretax account, which means that you don't pay federal taxes on money you put into it (although the Roth 401(k) is becoming more widely available).

- Pros: Often automatic and managed by a third party, frequently comes with employer match, high annual contribution limit ($23,500 in 2025).
- Cons: Less flexibility with investment choices, cumbersome to roll over when moving companies, potentially high expense ratios.
- Note that different types of organizations may have their own versions of the 401(k), but they essentially have the same function with different rules. The variations of all accounts will not be discussed in detail, so be sure to do your research and speak to your service provider for the specific account that you have.
  - 403(b): Often referred to as a tax-sheltered annuity plan (TSA), a 403(b) is a popular retirement plan for public education organizations and some health care service organizations in the United States. The contribution limit is generally the same as 401(k), and it has similar tax benefits.
  - 457(b): Commonly offered to state and local government employees and nonprofit employees. They are tax-deferred with similar benefits to a 401(k).

- ○ 401(a): This is a tax-advantaged account used for employees in government agencies, educational institutions, and nonprofit organizations.
- ○ Thrift Savings Plan (TSP): Another pretax vehicle that is utilized by federal employees.

The Ineffectiveness of the Catch-Up Contribution

The catch-up contribution is extra money that you can contribute to tax-advantaged accounts once you reach a certain age, currently 50+. Those who meet the age requirement are eligible to contribute an extra $7,500 to 401(k) and similar accounts, and $1,000 to the Roth IRA. For this discussion, we will focus on the $7,500 for the 401(k) since it is far more substantial than the $1,000 Roth IRA catch-up. Note that the Secure Act 2.0 requires high earners (>$145k/year) to contribute their 401(k) catch-ups to their Roth 401(k).

The bottom line is the importance of starting early and not relying on catch-up contributions to get you to your retirement goals. Catch-up contributions will barely move the needle in your retirement.

Is it better than nothing? Yes, but usually the people who need to utilize catch-up contributions are people who haven't been able to save enough for retirement and are trying to "catch up." Folks in this group are likely not maxing out their tax-advantaged space as it is, so having more space to use is not going to help. The exception to this is if they have had huge career growth in the last 10 years of working that would allow them to contribute additional money to their savings. Regardless, the impact of the catch-up contribution is mathematically negligible. Under the assumption that the person maxing out their 401(k) + catch-up contribution would have already been maxing their standard 401(k), the difference is a measly 3.2% in ending account balance after 10 years of catch-up contributions. Consider the following scenarios that utilize a 35-year contribution period and a 7% inflation-adjusted growth rate. The catch-up contribution period is the last 10 years of contributions, if applicable (Table 8.2).

Table 8.2 The ineffectiveness of the catch-up contribution

	Total invested	Ending balance	Growth ratio
Standard max contribution	$822,500	$3,248,567	3.95
Max contribution with catch-up	$897,500	$3,352,190	3.74
Forward tiered with catch-up	$672,500	$1,918,783	2.85
Forward tiered no catch-up	$597,500	$1,815,159	3.04
Tiered reverse	$362,500	$2,117,720	5.84

The **growth ratio** is the ending balance divided by the total invested balance; higher is better. See Section "The Ineffectiveness of the Catch-Up Contribution" in the appendix for graph and inputs

You may be thinking that it's simply unrealistic to max out your 401(k) in the early stages of your career, and you would be correct. Let's look at a forward-tiered contribution starting at $5,500/year and increasing by $750/year until it reaches the current IRS maximum allowable contribution. Following that, the person will utilize the max catch-up contribution. The ending balance is $1.9M, or about $0.1M more than if the person had not utilized the catch-up contribution, yielding a 5.7% higher balance than without the catch-up. Utilizing the 4% drawdown rule in retirement, the $0.1M difference will allow you to draw down an additional $4,145/ year, or $345/month. It's not nothing, but it is not life-changing either.

Let's also look at a reverse-tiered contribution where you begin at the maximum IRS contribution of $23,500/year and *reduce* your contribution by $750/year. When the catch-up contribution comes in the last 10 years of your career, you stop contributing altogether until retirement. Your ending balance is still higher than the forward-tiered case that utilizes the full catch-up contribution ($2.1M vs. $1.9M). Not only is the ending value higher, but the total contribution is also significantly lower at $362k versus $672k. This reconfirms the power of utilizing compounding growth as early in your life as possible.

The purpose of this exercise is not to tell you that the catch-up contribution is bad or that you should not use it—you should absolutely utilize all the tax-advantaged space you can. Rather, it is to say that younger folks might plan to rely on the catch-up period to finish saving for retirement when, in reality, the money you contribute in your 50s will not have any time to work its compounding magic and, thus, will not have a significant impact on your retirement income. The moral of the story is to invest as much as possible as early as possible.

Understanding Policies and Terminology

The language used to describe retirement savings programs confuses a lot of people. Many employers offer a 401(k), which is a type of professionally managed account, and many employers also offer 401(k) matches. Just because an employer offers a 401(k) does not mean that they offer a match. Even if there is no match, it is still advantageous to contribute to your 401(k) since it is tax advantaged.

You are probably reading this section to understand company matches, so let's use some examples to talk about the language they use:

Example 1: "100% match up to 5% of salary" means that the company will match every dollar that you contribute up to 5% of your total salary. It does not mean it will match everything you put in or match your entire salary; for example, for an $80k salary, the company will match 100% of 5% of $80k, which is $1,600/year. You are certainly allowed to (and recommended to) contribute more than what your company matches, up to the annual IRS limit.

Example 2: "1:1 match up to 4% contributed, and 1:2 match for the next 4% contributed" means that the company will match you completely for the first 4% that you contribute, then match half of your contribution for the next 4% (i.e., their contribution is 2%). This results in a max of 6% match from the company but requires you to contribute 8%.

Example 3: "10% match on salary upon 2% contribution" means that you must contribute 2% of your salary in order to get a match, which is 10%. In this case, there is no tiered system. You must contribute 2% of your salary—1.9% will get you no match. The good news is that upon completion of your 2%, you will get the full match from your employer.

Note that the total combined contribution limit from both you and your employer is $70k/year for 2025. If you have more questions about your company's specific retirement savings systems, don't hesitate to reach out to HR at your company—they should be able to provide more information or point you in the right direction.

Not all 401(k) accounts are created equal. Most employers have a vesting period/schedule for your match. Vesting is when the contributions made by your employer toward your 401(k) are handed over to you over a period of time. Most employer vesting schedules are between 3 and 5 years, and vest a portion each year until the total amount is vested. Having a vesting schedule incentivizes employees to stay at the company for a given number of years before leaving, since if an employee leaves, they are only awarded their vested amount. However, your own contributions are vested immediately, so if you leave before your match vests, you are only surrendering your company's contribution and not your own contributions.

Rolling over Your 401(k) to an IRA

There may be a time in your life when you will move companies. However, your 401(k) will not follow you since the account is managed by your previous employer or their financial institution of choice. For most companies, they hold onto it and continue to manage it for a certain period of time. One of the downsides of this is that expense ratios for 401(k) management are generally higher than that of an IRA. Therefore, it may be advantageous to roll old 401(k) accounts into a single IRA to consolidate accounts since there will be no additional contributions for the life of the account. Initiating a rollover is fairly straightforward—all you need to do is contact your account manager via phone or online to initiate it. There are no tax implications if you roll into a Pretax IRA, since they are in the same tax-advantaged space. You may elect to roll your 401(k) into a Roth IRA to rebalance the portfolio by forcing yourself to pay taxes on the transferred balance in exchange for not having to pay taxes in the future. If you do this, you will have to pay income tax at your marginal tax rate; however, you will not pay an early withdrawal penalty.

Pretax Versus Roth: Which Is best?

By this point, it should be clear that any tax-advantaged space is better than a non–tax-advantaged space. Therefore, the focus of this discussion lies with the question: Should you opt to pay taxes now or later?

It is difficult to pinpoint the exact scenario in which it would be advantageous to invest in pretax versus Roth, but in general it comes down to your earnings today versus your withdrawal rate in the future. If you are in a higher tax bracket now and anticipate being in a lower tax bracket in retirement, then a pretax account is better for you. Saving on taxes now when you are in a higher tax bracket would be advantageous compared with saving taxes in the future when you will most likely already be in a lower tax bracket. Most people fall into this category because in your working years, you are earning money to save and typically paying for a mortgage and dependents. Your (hypothetical) kids might have expensive needs like college tuition, car insurance for young drivers, sports, guitar lessons, and so on. Assuming you maintain the same standard of living in retirement, your expenses should be lower than your current expenses, and therefore you will be in a lower income tax bracket in the future than you are today. However, if you anticipate your tax bracket to be higher in retirement, then you may want to consider prioritizing a Roth account. The Roth is a great place to start if you are a relatively low earner now. As your income grows throughout your career, you can begin to contribute more toward pretax accounts while keeping your Roth account as a nice financial base.

Keep in mind that every dollar contributed to your Roth is taxed at your marginal tax rate, but every dollar withdrawn from your pretax account in retirement is taxed as ordinary income, where your entire income is *not* subject to your marginal tax rate. If pretax withdrawals in retirement were taxed entirely at your marginal rate, then the pretax versus Roth would have identical mathematical outcomes, but because federal tax rates are progressive, the pretax account is a mathematical win a majority of the time if all other factors remain the same. However, it's extremely likely that the other factors will *not* remain the same; the standard deduction and other tax deductions in the future will push the edge more toward pretax, but the Roth will become advantageous if tax rate increases outpace the rate of inflation. Nobody knows what any of those things will look like in the future.

Although you might fall into an income category that shows that it's advantageous to utilize one account over another, it is important to diversify your tax-advantaged money into both pretax and Roth buckets. Most advisers recommend maxing out the pretax 401(k) ($23,500) and a Roth IRA ($7,000), which results in a 77/23 split. Of course, there are other factors to include, such as expense ratios of a 401(k) versus an IRA, which can push in Roth IRA's favor due to the savings gained by self-management. Lastly, it may be better for you psychologically to know that you will not be on the hook for any taxes during retirement, which is a huge benefit of Roth IRA.

Optimizing Asset Allocation

Now that you are saving a decent chunk of your cash and investing it in accounts you've set up, you may be wondering what the optimal asset allocation is. There is no "one size fits all" allocation. There are many dials you can adjust in your portfolio, such as the stock/bond distribution, pretax/Roth/taxable distributions, and asset-type distributions such as real estate or other types of investments like businesses.

Generally speaking, you should be more weighted toward stocks (in Index/Mutual Fund form) earlier in life, and more weighted toward bonds as you get closer to retirement. "But I don't want to have to manually manage that throughout my career!" Don't worry, almost all brokerages have the Target Date Funds that we discussed earlier, which automatically shift your stock-to-bond ratio as you near your desired retirement date. In general, picking TDFs with years that are closer to today are more conservative (more bonds), while TDFs that have years that are far in the future have a more aggressive profile (more stocks).

Note: If your portfolio drops too much for comfort when the market pulls back between 10% and 20% (known as a *correction*, whereas a 20% or greater drop is considered a recession), then your asset allocation is set to too risky of a profile. Above all else, the best investing strategy is to stay the course even when things don't look great.

Another level of complexity exists when considering investments: your tax strategy. As discussed in the Pretax versus Roth section, the tax code will greatly influence which is the best method for retirement. However, nobody knows what the tax code will look like decades from now, not even the federal government! In addition to the tax code, your income and spending habits will have an impact on your future marginal tax rate. In general, if you expect your income and expenses in retirement to be higher than they are today, the Roth is advantageous. If you expect your income and expenses to be lower in retirement, the Pretax is advantageous. However, both of those things can be skewed by changes in the tax code—and you truly don't know what expenses will pop up in retirement! Taxable accounts are advantageous because although you are taxed on your contributions, you are only subject to long-term capital gains taxes upon withdrawal. This results in withdrawals incurring a lower tax burden versus pretax accounts. Taxable accounts also have no age or contribution restrictions, making it powerful for people who want to retire early. Therefore, it is advantageous to have exposure to all three types of accounts, and when the time comes to begin drawing down from them, draw down strategically to maximize your take-home pay and minimize tax burden.

To complicate things further, you might consider an investment outside of the stock market at some point in your life. Such an example is real estate. Whether you plan to invest in non-stock things is not important to this discussion, but it's something you should consider when considering your overall tax burden and asset allocation.

Let's discuss some asset allocation philosophies. For this analysis, we will focus on mitigating unnecessary risk and minimizing tax burden. First, let's discuss the "optimal" allocation in each bucket: the stocks versus bonds bucket and the Pretax versus Roth bucket. Afterward, we will combine the two.

Stocks Versus Bonds

In general, stocks and bonds are opposites. Stocks have higher risks and higher historical returns, while bonds have lower risks and lower historical returns. Historically, bonds have done relatively well when stocks were down, and stocks have done well when bond yields were low. Without going into technical detail, we can generalize and state that stocks are more

Scott's Thoughts: Rebalancing Strategy

Rebalancing is not discussed in detail in this book, mainly because I don't think it is important for the early-career investor to think about rebalancing. There are complexities such as tax implications/strategies and other nuances that the average new investor needn't care about. While many rebalancing strategies involve selling one investment to purchase another, my strategy just changes the contribution buckets. For example, suppose I want a 90:10 U.S.-to-International split and I contribute to my stocks such that 90% of my contributions go to U.S. stocks and 10% go to international stocks. By the end of any given year, U.S. stocks have outperformed international stocks and my portfolio is now 92:8. Rather than selling some U.S. stocks and using that money to purchase international stocks, I would just slightly bump my contribution to international stocks slightly to perhaps 88:12 and keep it that way until my overall portfolio evens out back to 90:10.

It's not an exact science, and there is also something to be said for selling your winners to buy losers, which has been shown to be a statistically bad idea. In terms of adjusting contribution ratios, I typically adjust once a year, maybe twice a year if the market has been volatile, but it's never a top priority for me unless things get way out of whack. Besides, once you build a large enough portfolio, your monthly contributions won't meaningfully change your asset allocation anyways.

sporadic while bonds are more stable in nature. Therefore, it is logical to believe that a mix of the two will yield the best performing portfolio. If only it were that easy! It's important to define what is meant by "best performance." Is it the highest return? Or is it the most stability? Only you can answer these questions. If you don't plan on touching the money for a few decades, do you care if the swings are larger in exchange for a higher return? On the other hand, will you sleep better at night knowing that you are able to weather large swings in the market due to a high bond allocation? Again, only you can answer these questions. In general, people who are further from retirement should allocate the vast majority of their portfolio (>90%) to stocks. There are many philosophies out there that range from having a 30% bond allocation to no bond allocation, and the general rule of thumb[34] is [Bond Allocation %] = [your age]. However, there are now recommendations to have it as your age minus 10 or 20 due to increased life expectancy.

Studies show that a small exposure to bonds actually outperforms a 100% stock allocation in both growth and volatility, but the timelines of those studies have been cherry-picked for certain periods in history.

Pretax Versus Roth Tax Treatments

As discussed earlier, the Pretax (Traditional) and Roth accounts both have their pros and cons. The earlier parts of this book cover the differences between these buckets. In general, it is more beneficial to use the pretax bucket if you plan on having lower income in retirement than you have right now. If you plan on having a higher income in retirement, the Roth bucket is better. You may think that you have a clue about what your financial situation will be like 40 years from now, but odds are you don't. Therefore, it's good to have exposure to both. In general, lower income folks who are early in their careers benefit from Roth (since their marginal tax bracket is low) and folks who are high earners and save a lot of money can benefit more from pretax accounts. If you have the capability, it never hurts to reap the benefits of both.

So…What Should My Asset Allocation Be?

Now that we've discussed the two major technical factors relevant to your asset allocation, we can return to your risk tolerance, time horizon, and personal preferences. Personal finance is all about making financial moves that allow us to sleep soundly at night and continue to invest when the going gets tough. Therefore, the mathematically optimal allocation (according to "models") may not be the most optimal allocation for you. In general, here are some principles that will guide you toward your optimal asset allocation:

- Assets that produce relatively high income (i.e., bonds and dividend stocks) should be allocated in a tax-deferred account (such as a tax-advantaged account and not a standard brokerage).

- If you are just starting out in your career and are a relatively low earner, then you should prioritize your Roth accounts for now.
- High-growth assets such as stock ETFs should be allocated in a Roth account.
- Assets that you don't plan to touch for the longest time should be allocated to the Roth account. This is because in the drawdown order, the Roth is typically the last one that is touched. The reason is that a Roth account can easily be transferred to heirs due to tax simplicity, and it has no taxes associated with selling assets, so you want compound interest to work the longest on that account.
- Keep in mind that your overall asset allocation might include your cash savings and your home equity, among other assets. Your cash savings might include your emergency fund and/or cash for big purchases. In general, you should not consider your emergency fund as part of your investment allocation since it is static and shouldn't change based on total investment value (it is based on your expenses). Your cash for big purchases might be considered depending on how large it is. After reading this section, it is up to you to decide how you want to view your portfolio and what makes you feel comfortable.
- As you move closer to retirement, follow the bond allocation guideline as stated earlier.

Scott's Thoughts: Asset Allocation

To reiterate, your asset allocation will primarily depend on your personal risk tolerance and your time horizon for retirement. I have almost no bond exposure because I simply don't care about short-term fluctuations in the market. The risk does not bother me at all because I know that I will not need this money in the near future. My investment philosophy differs further from traditional advice when it comes to "timing the market." Traditional wisdom mandates not to time the market—have a rock-solid strategy that enables you to invest steadily through market downturns. While my personal strategy does invest through downturns, I turn the dial up on investments around 5% to

10% when the market isn't doing well. It's like buying groceries on sale and putting them in the freezer for the future! I never try to anticipate how long the market will be in a downturn, but I increase investments slightly during bear markets (e.g., 2022) so that when the market rebounds I can take advantage of purchasing stocks at a discount. On the contrary, I never sell when the market is up or decrease my base contributions. I will continue to invest when the market is at all-time highs. It is understandable that most people don't have an extra 5% to 10% to invest at any given time, but I lower my monthly cash savings and work with what I have—another reason why I like to keep more cash on hand than the average person.

Additionally, I am ok with the risk of selling stocks to purchase real estate. Of course, the deal has to make mathematical sense, but I am ok with saving up for real estate within a stock portfolio rather than a savings account. Saving for a personal home is different since that is a lifestyle choice rather than an investment choice, but using stocks to purchase an investment property is simply a portfolio shift from stock assets to real estate assets (with some taxes involved). I don't mind if stocks tank and I am unable to liquidate them to purchase an investment property; if stocks tank I simply continue to purchase stocks.

Think like an Investor

Understanding Your Risk Tolerance

Your risk tolerance is a combination of your *ability* to take risks and your *willingness* to take risks. Your ability to take risks is governed by your short-term and long-term financial goals. Perhaps you plan on saving money for a down payment on a home in the next couple years. That would limit your ability to use that money in higher risk investments such as stocks. A safe place for that money would be in a HYSA or perhaps some treasury bonds or CDs. The overall riskiness of your portfolio should be based on when you will need the money and how much of it you might need. It is a value that, while challenging to calculate, has a direct influence on your risk tolerance.

Your willingness to take risks is determined mainly by your psychological fortitude. If you are constantly worried that the market will tank and your investments will go down, you should de-risk your portfolio so that you can sleep better at night (health care is expensive!) and avoid irrational adjustments to your portfolio. Being invested in high-risk, high-return assets doesn't mean anything if you can't stay the course or are losing sleep over it.

Balance can be achieved by adjusting the stocks and bonds asset allocation, as discussed in the previous section. A higher portion of stocks will lead to a riskier portfolio while a higher portion of bonds will lead to a safer portfolio. Generally, growth potential is the trade-off with increased safety.

The other factor that you must consider is your desire for portfolio growth versus preservation. While this is typically correlated with age or retirement status, your appetite for growth versus preservation might be different depending on your financial status and plans for where your money might go after you are gone. For example, if you have much more than you need for retirement, you may only need to withdraw 2% of your portfolio annually to survive. Therefore, you might be able to have more growth positions in your portfolio that might be able to weather more swings (by the time you reach the recommended 4% withdrawal rate, your portfolio would have had to have fallen 50%!). On the flipside, if you are looking to die with nothing and barely have enough money to survive until then, you might consider a portfolio that is focused on preservation. This will allow your portfolio to weather storms with greater certainty until the moment you don't need it anymore.

A short discussion on loss aversion: The concept of loss aversion has been studied extensively by behavioral economists and made famous by Israeli American psychologist Daniel Kahneman in *Thinking Fast and Slow*. Loss aversion is the phenomenon wherein people respond to losses more strongly than they respond to corresponding gains. It is a cognitive bias that makes people tend toward the idea that losses loom larger than gains. In terms of investing, loss aversion indicates that most people lean toward a slightly smaller rate of return in exchange for greatly reduced odds of losing large amounts of money, even if the potential for gains is equally high.

Scott's Thoughts: Early-Career Investment Risks

If you cannot learn from others' mistakes, it is best to learn and make investment mistakes early in your career. I made plenty of investing mistakes when my portfolio was a fraction of what it is today. I invested too much in individual stocks, followed market hype, succumbed to investment FOMO (fear of missing out), and got roped into yield trap dividend stocks. I lost, at the time, what seemed like a lot of money. As my portfolio grew, my financial maturity grew and my ability to withstand fluctuations in the market improved. Now, I can sit still in the market and keep cool while doing it. The amount that my portfolio swings in a single day in a volatile market is equivalent to the amount of money I gained or lost in an entire year in my early days of investing. The psychological toughness of investing can only be learned through real-world experience—while you can learn what it takes to be a fast runner, you cannot acquire the grit needed to run fast by simply putting on sneakers and looking at a treadmill. I am not referring to the mental toughness of making trade after trade like a hedge fund investor on Wall Street; I'm talking about watching a 25% bear market sink your portfolio by half your annual salary and keeping cool knowing that it's going to be alright as long as you stay the course. Zoom out on any S&P 500 chart, and you'll see that events that we once saw as major catastrophes in the market have all faded into blips in the investment timeline. After having made many errors that I have chalked up to the cost of learning, I will make far fewer errors in future investments. Since my portfolio is now significantly larger, the stakes are much higher, but my mental toughness is stronger too.

Following Your Investment Principles

Investing for your future can be a nerve-racking prospect, since the market can fluctuate a lot in a single year. However, it is important to stick to your guns and not let short-term fluctuations sway you from your long-term goals. You will hear a lot of "the market is down so I am going to take my money out and invest when it's lower" or "the market is doing well so I am going to invest more!" On the contrary, you'll never hear, "I hate buying groceries when they're on sale, I'd rather buy groceries when they go up in price!" Having a solid, simple investment strategy that you stick to regardless of market conditions is going to do more for your financial future than anything else!

You may still be nervous about investing your hard-earned money, no matter how diversified it may be. Given the recent economic events, that is understandable. You may have heard folks say, "I don't want to invest now because what if the market goes down?" I always respond with "What if you don't invest and the market goes up?" In the years 1970 to 2024, the market ended lower than it started for 11 of the 54 years. Those are pretty good odds if you ask me!

The market is constantly reaching "all-time highs." Look back at zoomed-out graph of the market over the last 50+ years. You will see hundreds of "all-time highs," and each time one is reached, it is subsequently surpassed. If the market falls in such a way that millions of Americans' livelihoods are drastically impacted and stays that way for an extended period, then there will be much bigger problems than our silly investments.

Your goal should be to develop an investment philosophy that you can and will follow regardless of economic conditions. Some things that may sway your philosophy or strategy are changes to the tax code, changes to your future personal needs, or changes to economic policy. Aside from these things, you want to make sure your strategy is rock solid. You should not fiddle around with your investments for the sake of feeling like you're doing something—a watched pot never boils! Have you ever heard the saying, "Don't just stand there, do something!"? Well, in investing, the saying is, "Don't do anything, just stand there!" A good litmus test for your investment strategy is to ask yourself, "If I automate everything right now and I lose Internet access for the next 5 years, will I be ok with my strategy?"

Understand that a rock-solid strategy does not need to be complicated. It can be as simple as, for example, "buy $1,500 of VTSAX or equivalent U.S. total market fund every month in my pretax 401(k) and max out my Roth IRA with half VOO and half VXUS every year." The simpler your investment strategy, the easier it is to follow, understand, manage, and make changes in the future. Do not believe it when people tell you that you need to implement complicated investment strategies.

Odds are they want to charge you thousands of dollars per year to help you with those strategies. Note that even if they did outperform the market (less than 14%[35] of professional investors consistently beat the market over a 20-year period), you would still have to pay them, which negates the advantage of hiring a professional!

Warren Buffet has stated that when he passes, his estate will be executed in the following way: Donate "a vast majority" to charity, place 90% of what's left into an S&P 500 index fund such as VOO, and hold indefinitely. Presumably the last 10% will be cash or a similar type of holding. The most successful investor of all time (Net Worth: $141 billion as of 2025) has designated a simple two lines of instruction to invest the remaining billions of dollars he has. Your strategy doesn't need to be more complex than that.

The Sunk Cost Fallacy

If you have ever thought, "This is not beneficial at all, but I've already come this far, so might as well see it through," then you have experienced the sunk cost fallacy. The sunk cost fallacy is *the phenomenon whereby a person is reluctant to abandon a strategy or course of action because they have invested heavily into it, even when it is clear that abandonment would be more beneficial.* This can happen to people often in daily life, but it is also prominent in many people's investment strategies. You may have investments in your portfolio that are "dead" or a suboptimal asset allocation or fund selection. The sunk cost fallacy is the ideology that you should not do anything with those investments because you already made the decision to purchase them. As a young professional, making the proper changes to your portfolio can have a massive impact on your future financial health. Even if you are near retirement, it is never too late to make changes.

Here are two simple ways to rebalance your portfolio when trying to avoid the sunk cost fallacy. The first way is simply to sell the non-optimal assets and repurchase the optimal assets. There are some *tax loss harvesting* strategies that you can implement, which is essentially when you use the losses from sale of an investment to offset gains from another. The second method is simply to add to your portfolio until it reaches the optimal level. This only works if your allocation is incorrect but your fund choice is correct. For example, you have 20% of your investments in individual stocks but learned recently that it's too risky and want to decrease allocation to 5%. You might sell half of your stocks for tax loss harvesting and then add other assets to your portfolio to dilute your remaining 10% until it reaches 5% of your total portfolio.

Here is a tip to help you avoid the sunk cost fallacy. Suppose you have $1,000 worth of Stock A. You're down some money, but you're afraid that selling it will "solidify" that loss. If you did not own Stock A today, but were given $1,000, would you invest it elsewhere or purchase $1,000 worth of Stock A? If you answered "invest elsewhere," then you have determined that your best course of action is to sell and use the money elsewhere. If you chose not to sell, then you have fallen prey to the sunk cost fallacy.

The same logic applies to your overall personal finance strategy. You likely have some sort of financial organization like bank or investment accounts, a budget, automated savings, and so on. It's easy to say, "I've done it this way for my entire life, so I am going to continue doing it this way." To avoid falling into the sunk cost fallacy, it is important to ask yourself: If you started your financial journey from scratch with what you know today, how would you structure your investments? Then you are able to get rid of what you don't need and implement what you do.

The Impacts of Politics to Investments

You may be thinking, "How has he managed to avoid talking about politics up until now?" The reason is that in the grand scheme of things, the political party or sitting president generally does not matter in your personal finances. There have been bear and bull markets in both Republican- and Democrat-run offices. There have been periods of high and low inflation and unemployment from both political parties. Show anyone a dateless graph of the any of the aforementioned items and ask them to point out whether the president was a Democrat or Republican during any given section, and they likely won't be able to. This isn't to say that politics has no impact to the economy, as it certainly does. This is to say that a properly set up personal finance strategy is nearly immune to changes in the political climate. Will you have to adjust when market and economic conditions change? Yes! Will there be good times and bad times from both political parties that you will need to navigate through in your lifetime? Yes! Can you and your investments grow financially regardless of who is in office? Yes! Do not let the media or anyone brainwash you into thinking that you cannot be financially successful because your preferred political party isn't in office at the moment.

"God, grant me the serenity to accept the things I cannot change, the courage to change the things I can, and the wisdom to know the difference."—Serenity Prayer. Take control of the things that you can, such as your budget, job, professional education and training, savings and spending habits, investment contributions, emergency fund amount, debt holdings, and so on and use those things, along with your knowledge, to prepare adequately for the things that you cannot control such as market returns, inflation rates, unemployment, interest rates, and so on.

The Bottom Line

If you have read this entire investment section and are still overwhelmed, fear not. In this section, I will list the most fundamental steps you need to take to get started. Remember that **you do not need a perfect investment strategy from the start**. Do not get hung up on VOO versus VTI; mutual funds versus ETFs; whether you should include international and bond funds and at what percentages; qualified dividends versus nonqualified dividends; Roth versus pretax allocation; how you should taper your investments starting 15 years from retirement; Fidelity versus Vanguard; the types of bonds you're investing in; the cost basis of your portfolio; and so on. For the time being, *none of those things matter as much as your savings rate and habits*.

As a young professional, you should be developing the habit of consistently saving and investing rather than stressing about how to do so. Alongside, you will develop the emotional and psychological capacity to deal with swings in your portfolio value—a valuable skill to have as your portfolio grows larger. **As long as you are saving the right percentage of your paycheck, everything you do after that is simply optimization in the short term.** You have decades of investment time ahead of you—suboptimal investing for the first few months or even years is not going to ruin your financial future. You may realize several years from today that an 80/20 stock-to-bond split was better for you than the 90/10 split that you had started with. It is far better to adjust than to have not invested at all. Do not let analysis paralysis stop you from going out and getting started. Let's summarize:

1. Open a brokerage account (preferably a Roth IRA if you are not a high earner yet) and link it with your main checking account
   a. You can open a Roth IRA and a regular taxable account at the same brokerage company to keep everything organized and streamlined
2. Set your account of choice to transfer money monthly from your checking account to your brokerage account
   a. Observe the annual contribution limit for the IRA
   b. There is no contribution limit for a regular taxable brokerage account
3. Set your account to purchase your fund(s) of choice each month or in a lump sum.
   a. Choice 1: "aggressive" (80%–90% VTI, 10% VXUS, 0%–10% BND)
      i. Best for 15+ years from retirement
   b. Choice 2: "moderate" (65%–80% VTI, 10% VXUS, 10%–25% BND)
      i. Best for 10 to 15 years from retirement
   c. Choice 3: "conservative" (50%–65% VTI, 10% VXUS, 25%–40% BND)
      i. Best for <10 years from retirement
4. Leave it alone and let compound growth do its thing

CHAPTER 9

Retirement

Defining Retirement

Retirement is the largest purchase of your entire life. It is when you take the money you've saved up and buy back the working years of your life so that you don't have to work anymore. Rather than trading your time for money, you are now trading your money for time. Throughout your life thus far, you have been in the accumulation phase. Now, it is time to transition to the drawdown/preservation phase. Retirement can look very different to various people, so it's important to accurately prioritize your wants, needs, and time! Keep in mind that retirement is not an age but a financial status. Someone who is 40 years old with $3M in savings/investments might be able to retire even though they are not of the traditional retirement age, whereas someone who is 67 who only has $50k in savings/investments might have to work for the rest of their life.

There are gray areas between working full time and a full-on retirement. One may become financially independent and choose to take a lower paying job that has more flexible hours and stop contributing to their retirement accounts and have more money to travel while they're still young and able to move. The reality is that money provides people with flexibility and financial independence, not just "retirement."

In your mind, you may be thinking that "life is short" and "why should I save for retirement if there's going to be Social Security?" Let me start by saying that very few people regret saving too much for retirement (most of those people end up retiring a few years early or upgrading their lifestyle later in life), but you meet people every day who regret not saving enough. Also, keep in mind that Social Security is intended to provide the bare minimum income required to survive in society. The worst-case scenario if someone retires early and begins to run out of money is that they go back to work to supplement their investment income and Social

Security. The worst-case scenario of not saving enough and retiring late is that you never get to enjoy the golden years of your life.

As of 2022, the average retirement age is around 61 years old,[36] and the average life expectancy is 76 years old.[37] On average, that's 15 years to enjoy the fruits of your labor.

FIRE and Relevant Principles

FIRE stands for Financial Independence, Retire Early. Before we get started, let's discuss the philosophy of retirement in more detail. In an earlier section, we defined retirement as being a financial state and not an age. A 40-year-old with $3M saved up might be able to easily retire while a 67-year-old with $50k might barely be able to retire. FIRE has taken the world by storm—for a good reason! People are not interested in working until they are too old to move *and* lack confidence in the Social Security system in the decades to come. While nobody can comment on whether Social Security will still be around decades from now, we must still consider and prepare for both possibilities.

The premise of FIRE is that if you retire early and begin to run out of money, you can reenter the workforce for supplemental income, even if it's not a high-paying job. If you retire late, there is no turning back from that. If you find that you saved too much money for retirement (what a nice problem to have), then you can simply choose to retire a few years earlier than the average American (which would still be considered FIRE)! Note that the current average age of retirement is 61 in the United States.

FI Before RE

FIRE is a two-step process. First, you gain financial independence from the daily work grind. Then, you retire early from the workforce. You do not have to attain FI and RE simultaneously. In fact, when you attain FI, you can choose to continue working until traditional retirement age. Many people who become financially independent shift to less stressful jobs, which allow better work–life balance, more flexible work locations, and more fulfilling work. Financial independence is when you do not need to rely on an employer for your next paycheck. The idea is that you do not have to jump through hoops to satisfy your supervisor or make money for the company you work for. This is not to say you shouldn't take pride in your own career and growth! It's about being able to work and grow on your own terms since you are not relying on your next paycheck, or any paycheck for that matter.

There are many types[38] of FIRE that will not be covered in this book. Overall, you should ask yourself what type of lifestyle you'd want if you didn't have a job and whether you'd like to continue working in your industry after becoming financially independent.

There is no "how-to" for this section; it's mainly to place the idea of financial freedom in your mind and perhaps move you toward FIRE. Keep in mind that retiring early doesn't necessarily mean retiring at 35 and traveling the world. That is an unrealistic expectation that is only for a minuscule portion of the population (far less than 1%). It can simply mean becoming financially independent at 50, taking a less stressful and lower paying job until 55, and retiring 6 years earlier than the average American, or spending more time with family and friends rather than being in the office 40 to 50 hours per week. Not only does having financial independence make your life less stressful, it also allows you to become involved in your family, philanthropy, and your hobbies. It is a win-win for all.

The Levels of Financial Independence

There are varying levels of financial independence, and they are all categorized differently. Financial independence ranges from living just above paycheck to paycheck to being able to do whatever you want with your time and life. It takes years (or a large windfall of cash) to move from the bottom tier to the top tier of financial independence. While the levels don't necessarily have hard lines, they are small wins that progressively have larger and larger impacts to your overall quality of life.

1. FI from credit cards: Once you no longer require a credit card or any sort of short-term loan to go about your day-to-day living, you are considered FI from credit cards. Being FI from credit cards doesn't mean that you don't use credit cards anymore (frankly you

should use your credit card whenever you can), just that you are not relying on the card to pay for regular expenses or are unable to pay at the end of the month. Ultimately, relying on credit cards, rather than using them strategically, means you are still borrowing from your future self to pay your present self.

2. FI from the average emergency: The average financial emergency in the United States is around $1,700, which means that if you have $1,700 in your savings account, you are able to accommodate most emergencies that pop up in your life (e.g., emergency room visits, insurance deductibles on your vehicle, vet visits for your pet, spilled coffee on your laptop, etc.). Having this security net in your savings account will enable you not to go into high-interest debt to stay afloat, which means that you will not disturb the rest of your financial system when emergencies happen.

3. FI from job loss: The next step in your financial independence journey is to accumulate a 3 to 6-month emergency fund, which will protect you in the event that you lose your job or need to take unpaid leave for any reason. This will also allow you to spend time searching for your next job without having to take the first thing that comes across your plate. You want to make sure that your next job is fulfilling, rewarding, and has adequate compensation before accepting it, and having an emergency fund is the way to do that. In addition to job loss, your 3 to 6-month emergency fund will also cover much larger non–job-related emergencies.

4. FI from your job: The step after being able to easily weather a lay-off is being able to choose when you take time off. Suppose you feel that you want to spend a year off with your newborn child or just take a year off of work to travel. Being completely financially independent from your job is critical to being able to do that. It also means that not only are your investments for your actual retirement in good standing but you also have a reserve fund for said sabbatical. During this time, you might not be able to continue to save, but you may be able to live off your reserve fund and dividends from your investments.

5. FI for life, or true F-U money: This is when your investments can subsidize 100% of your annual expenses and you don't need to work ever again. Typically, this is when your invested total reaches

approximately 25 times your annual expenses, which allows you to draw down 4% of your well-balanced portfolio and adjust for inflation each year with virtually zero risk of ever running out of money. If you reach this point, you are truly able to tell your boss to pound sand if you don't feel like working anymore. Alternatively, you can work a small job for some income to supplement your lifestyle.

Retrieving Tax-Advantaged Money Early

There is a common misconception that once you put money into a tax-advantaged account, the money is "locked away until you're 60." That is not true, and it costs people thousands of dollars in taxes every year when they utilize taxable accounts or use it as an excuse to not save anything at all. There are a variety of methods to access your tax-advantaged money early, albeit with some planning required. In general, accessing tax-advantaged money has to be done for the right reasons. If you are accessing money to pay off debt, then you are forgoing all future growth potential of the money. In no particular order, here are the most common methods.

Eating the Penalties

Withdrawing your money from a pretax retirement account will subject you to federal income tax in your current income bracket, and a 10% early withdrawal penalty. This is the reason why some people incorrectly advocate for not contributing as much as possible to your 401(k). The 10% penalty for early withdrawal may sting, but it is not as mathematically inefficient as you might think when used properly. If you withdraw early from your 401(k) while working full time, your tax liability is your marginal federal rate + a 10% penalty. However, if you are in a position to retire early, you are no longer receiving income and the ability for you to retire early means that your core expenses are much lower than your overall income. Therefore, if you withdraw from your 401(k) early, your marginal tax rate might be 12% or you may bleed into the 22% a bit. After the standard deduction, there is high likelihood that you will end up in a lower tax bracket. If you are in a position to retire early, the 10% penalty isn't the end of the world as long as your retirement tax bracket isn't terribly high. If you are retiring early, then your marginal tax bracket while working is likely higher than what it would be if you were retired and withdrawing from your account to pay your expenses only.

Roth Conversion Ladder

The Roth IRA is an amazing investment vehicle, because it not only allows you to contribute a certain amount per year on which you will not need to pay capital gains taxes, but you may also roll over other investment vehicles into this account with no limit. Recall that rollovers into a Roth require a 5-year "seasoning" period. For example, you may roll over an entire 401(k) account with $100k in value into your Roth IRA. Since you are rolling a pretax account into a Roth account, the amount that you rollover is subject to income tax but NOT the 10% penalty. After the 5-year seasoning period, you can withdraw the entire amount. Because of the seasoning period, it is advantageous to utilize a *ladder* approach, which involves rolling over your estimated annual expense into your Roth IRA 5 years ahead of schedule, and repeating the rollover each year until you retire and then continuing to utilize the ladder into retirement until you reach eligible retirement age. This is advantageous because you spread out your tax burden to lower brackets. Rather than paying tax in the 24% marginal bracket with a $100k withdrawal, you may only need $50k/year to live and pay tax in the 12% bracket annually. The downside is that you need to understand your expenses 5 years into the future with reasonable accuracy, and any additional income in that 5-year seasoning period requires you to pay marginal taxes on that. Even if you don't create a perfect plan, you can supplement your withdrawals with other forms of income such as a standard taxable brokerage or real estate, another reason to have income and tax strategy diversification as you grow closer to retirement!

SEPP Distribution (72T)

The SEPP (substantially equal periodic payments) distribution is relatively self-explanatory. The premise is that you determine a fixed amount you want to withdraw from your pretax account. You withdraw this amount each year and pay regular federal income taxes on it. The caveat is that this amount is fixed and you must take this withdrawal until you reach retirement age. While it's less complicated than the Roth conversion ladder, it provides no flexibility to your retirement plan.

Qualified Withdrawals

Also known as "exceptions," there are several instances in which you are allowed to withdraw a portion of your IRA contributions penalty-free. One situation is if you were to use that money to purchase a home. However, there are some caveats. First, the withdrawal limit is $10,000 per person, and that is a lifetime limit. This means that you could withdraw $6,000 and $4,000 separately at different points in your life. Secondly, you must be a "first-time homebuyer." This does not mean that it's your first home—you must "have never owned a home or a primary residence for at least two years." For example, if you withdraw $6,000 to purchase your first home in 2025 and live there until 2030, then decide to rent from 2030 to 2033 and then purchase another home, you are eligible to utilize the $4,000 to make a total of $10,000.

Another exception is using funds from your IRA to pay for unreimbursed medical expenses that exceed 7.5% of your adjusted gross income. However, the medical bills have to be pretty substantial in order for this to come into effect. Therefore, this type of withdrawal is called a hardship withdrawal.

Conclusion

Ultimately, there are a couple of ways to retrieve tax-advantaged money early. Although they may require some legwork beyond just hitting the withdraw button, they can save you a large chunk of change and put you in direct control of your retirement funds. Most importantly, understanding your future lifestyle and having realistic expectations around your expenses and spending are going to be the biggest determining factor as to which method or combination of methods is suitable for you.

Calculations for a Traditional Retirement

There is a plethora of retirement calculations that help you determine how much you'll need invested to retire. If you do not plan on relying on Social Security or a pension, the calculations are relatively straightforward. However, accepting money at various dates and in varying amounts can complicate your strategy. The baseline strategy is that you save 25 times your current expenses and draw your portfolio down around 4% per year.

For example, if your current expenses are $60k/year, you need 25 × 60k = $1.5M to comfortably retire. Drawing down your $1.5M at 4% per year will yield $60k. Note that you will be taxed on a portion of this income, so you may need to adjust accordingly. In order to see if your contributions will end up at $1.5M in, say 30 years, you can use a calculator such as this online[39] one. Starting at $0 and saving $15k/year at 7% compounding yields $1.42M after 30 years. Since 30 years is a long time, you should test a lower and higher rate of return. A return of 6% and 8% gives ending values of $1.19M and $1.70M, respectively. For a 7% rate of return, your options are either to work slightly longer (31 years at 7% and $15k/year gets you to $1.53M) or contribute slightly more annually (30 years at 7% and $16k/year gets you to $1.51M).

As you get closer to retirement, you can hone your numbers and see if you'll need to work longer. Luckily, you won't have to take wild guesses at future returns or expenses anymore because will be closer to retirement. As discussed in the Catch-Up Contribution section, contributing more when you're closer to retirement unfortunately will not make nearly as big an impact as contributing early in your career. Oftentimes, the only choice is to work longer, which reiterates the importance of getting started on saving and investing as early as possible.

There are two main ways to view retirement drawdown: total amount invested and total monthly income. Both will yield the same answer. The example provided was based on the total amount invested. However, it's challenging to take into account Social Security or Pension payments via the total amount invested since you don't know the equivalent value of your monthly payments. Fortunately, you know the 4% rule or 25× rule. You can easily take your monthly Social Security benefit and multiply by 25 to figure out the "total value" of your Social Security. Suppose your monthly SS benefits are $1,500/month or $18,000/year. That is the equivalent of $18k × 25 = $450k lump sum withdrawn at 4%. In this case, if you have $800k saved up in your 401(k), you can say that you have the equivalent of approximately $1.25M available for retirement at a steady withdrawal rate.

The other method is the monthly or annual payment method. It considers monthly payments and potential monthly payments from all of your retirement sources. If your $800k portfolio pays you $32k/year and SS pays you $18k/year, your total annual income will be $50k or $4,167 per month. It's really just two sides of the same coin—you can use whichever philosophy you'd like!

Note that the annual viewpoint makes it easier to calculate tax burden in retirement.

Drawdown Rate Discussion

The 4% rule is based on historical market performance of a 50/50 stock/bond split over a 30-year period. The basis is that you withdraw 4% of your total portfolio for the first year of retirement, and every year thereafter you increase your withdrawal by the rate of inflation. You do not always draw down 4% of your entire portfolio. The success rate of this rule is above 99%. Some critics suggest a more conservative 3% to 3.5% withdrawal rate while optimistic folks say 5% is acceptable as long as you trim down spending during economic downturns. In reality, the 4% rule study was done in a static environment; it assumes that the person drawing down from their portfolio draws the same amount each year, adjusted for inflation. In reality, it would be wise to draw slightly less when the market is trending down and draw slightly more when the market is trending up—and save the excess withdrawals as cash in a savings account for a rainy day. Additionally, the 4% rule does not consider fixed income from other sources such as Social Security, a pension, or even an inheritance as some people receive later in their lives. Your spending will vary from year to year in retirement and you want to understand it, reiterating the importance of budgeting and tracking your spending.

Technically, the act of withdrawing more cash when the market is up and withdrawing less cash when the market is down is a form of timing the market, which is generally frowned upon. However, it offers a small cash reserve edge when the market is up and will allow you to not draw down as much when the market is down. This is another reason for having a minimum of 1 year, or ideally 3 years, of emergency cash on hand during retirement.

Social Security

You may have heard of this thing called "Social Security." Most people only know that it's going to give you some amount of money for your retirement, but the way it works is quite complicated. You can read more about Social Security at the official website,[40] but the gist is this:

- You pay a total of 15.3% of your gross income toward the FICA tax (Federal Insurance Contributions Act).
  - Your employer pays half of it (for W2 employees only, 1099 employees are required to pay the entire amount themselves).
- The half that you pay (7.65%) is split into two portions: 6.2% toward Social Security Tax, and 1.45% toward Medicare Tax.
  - Since Social Security tax is a regressive tax, single filers are only taxed on the first $176,100 of income in 2025.
- The money that everybody pools into the system is then distributed to folks who are already retired and eligible to collect.
- The government keeps track, via your tax records, of your contributions and you earn credits for Social Security Benefits.
  - You must work for at least 10 years (40 credits) to qualify for benefits.
  - Your benefits are based on your highest 35 years of income.
- You can go online to calculate your benefits using the quick calculator[41] or the advanced calculator.[42]

There are many schools of thought when it comes to whether to rely on Social Security as a source of income in retirement. We will not discuss the likelihood of Social Security's existence in the future since nobody knows the answer for sure, but what we do know is that we should know how to handle multiple scenarios in the event of changes to the Social Security system. A conservative philosophy is not to include Social Security benefits in your retirement calculations. A more aggressive approach is to use your estimated future income to calculate your benefits and use that as your income during your retirement. A moderate approach would be to use half of your estimated benefits—the average of the two philosophies. Nonetheless, the Social Security system is something that you must pay into and is something you may want to take into consideration when planning your finances.

The Pension

A pension[43] is sort of like Social Security but internal to your company. You and/or your employer contribute to it, and upon retirement you receive benefits. Many pension plans have requirements as to how long you must have worked at the company and minimum age before withdrawal. Each company's policies are different. In general, pensions are being phased out and replaced with 401(k)s. Pensions are sometimes not very clear to many folks. There are formulas that you can use to calculate how much you have in your pension and how it's going to grow over time. Nonetheless, a pension is still a valuable tool in your retirement toolbox. The best place to learn about your company's pension is through your company's benefits page or HR. A standard pension benefit might look something like this:

- You contribute X% of your pay for Y years (optional as some pension plans are fully company-sponsored).
- Your retirement benefit is some portion of your average salary for the last B years of working at the company, multiplied by C number of years that you have worked at the company (or a percentage that is essentially a vesting percentage).
  - For example, you work with the company for 15 years but you need 20 years to fully vest so you get 75% of the full benefit, which is 50% of your average pay in the last 5 years of working. Your last 5 years you averaged $100k/year, so you will get 75% of 50% of $100k each year in retirement, so $37.5k/year.
- Note that pension payouts generally have to do with current interest rates.
  - In general, the value of a lump sum pension is inversely related to the interest rates. When interest rates rise, the present value of future pension payments decreases. This leads to a lower

lump sum value. When rates fall, the present value of future pension payments increases. This leads to a higher lump sum value.

- In general, you don't really need to consider the implications of interest rates on your pension until you are nearing retirement, as nobody knows what rates will do in the future.

Retirement Checklist

In order to prepare for retirement, you should look at or do the following things:

- Balloon your cash emergency fund to a minimum of 1 year of cash and ideally 3 years.
  - This will no longer be considered strictly an emergency fund, but rather floating cash. It puts a buffer between your day-to-day expenses and your investments. This will allow you to ride out small bear markets and simultaneously not dip into your investments too much when an emergency occurs.
  - Having a large buffer also allows you to optimize your tax strategy by choosing when and where to withdraw money.
- If you haven't already done this, track your expenses for at least a year.
  - Be realistic about what you will spend in retirement—keep in mind that having an extra 40 to 50 hours per week means more time to spend money and do things, even if they're relatively inexpensive hobbies like gardening. On the other hand, your transportation costs may go down since you will not have to commute to work.
  - You also want to understand the tax implications of withdrawing from various accounts. Talk to a CPA if you are unsure. It is totally possible that you will end up paying very little in taxes if your accounts are set up properly.
- Pay off all debt that isn't your mortgage. If possible, pay off your mortgage too unless it's extremely low interest.

- ○ It is not a requirement not to have a mortgage in retirement, but it certainly de-risks your life by having lower baseline expenses.
- ○ Aside from ultra-low-interest debt, you really should not carry any consumer debt, such as car loans, into retirement. Keep in mind that the more debt you have, the more you have to withdraw from your retirement accounts to pay it back, and thereby incur greater taxes.
- Understand the cost of health insurance—healthcare can be way more expensive than you think, so be sure to get several quotes ahead of time.
  - ○ If possible, get your expensive appointments, treatments, and medications out of the way while you are still on employer health insurance.
- Make sure your asset allocation is correct for your risk tolerance and age.
  - ○ A rough rule of thumb is to have your stock/bond allocation where your bond percentage is approximately your age. In other words, the older and closer to retirement you get, the more conservative your portfolio will become. Guaranteed income such as pension and Social Security can be considered "bond" allocation because the risk is essentially zero.
- Make sure that you have proper term life insurance policies in place if you have people who still depend on your income.

CHAPTER 10

The Homebuying Process

Shopping for and purchasing a home will likely be one of the most financially stressful moments of your entire life, which makes sense—it will likely be the biggest purchase of your life thus far. Embarking on the journey of homebuying is best done when you are equipped with the basic tools. The purpose of this section is not to tell you how to do everything, but rather what to consider, how these things might affect the bottom line, and what metaphorical levers to pull to move yourself in the right direction. We will not cover exactly how to execute the homebuying process, just things you should consider throughout the process.

Financing Your Home

The Loan

There are multiple ways to finance a home. What you use will depend on your needs, income, credit score, and situation. Let's go through each loan type and the fundamentals of each.

Conventional: This popular type of loan usually requires 20% down for single-unit primary residences. Less than 20% and you may have to pay private mortgage insurance (PMI). Typically, the lowest you can put down on a conventional loan is 5%, although some lenders now allow 3%. There are a variety of ways to remove PMI from the loan without refinancing, which makes conventional the best option. Note that if you are purchasing a duplex or multifamily property, you generally must put down 15% to 25% depending on the number of units, even if it will be your primary residence.

FHA (Federal Housing Administration) Loan: This loan is meant for borrowers who have lower income and credit scores since the loan is insured by the government. A benefit of the FHA loan is that you can put only 3.5% down and the loan can be used for noncommercial multifamily properties up to four units. Note that the multifamily units have financing rules[44] associated with them. The downside to the FHA loan is the Mortgage Insurance Premium (MIP[45]) which has both an upfront cost and monthly cost. Unlike PMI, MIP lasts 11 years (when putting >10% down) or the life of the loan (when putting <10% down). You cannot remove lifetime MIP unless you refinance to a conventional mortgage.

Cash: Using cash is the most straightforward way to purchase a home. It cuts down on closing costs, closing time, and increases your chances of getting the deal. The downside is that it is incredibly hard as a young professional to have enough cash to purchase a home outright.

Adjustable Rate Mortgage (ARM): They have fixed rates for the first few years, then adjust every so often according to the loan terms. Oftentimes, variable interest loans can have lower upfront interest rates but higher risk due to the potential for rate increases in the future. ARM loans are not intrinsically bad and can be a useful tool under the right conditions. Let's look at a few examples:

- ARM 5/1—fixed rate for 5 years and then adjusts every 1 year after that
- ARM 7/6—fixed rate for 7 years and then adjusts every 6 months after that
- Note that ARMs sometimes have limits for how much the rates can move in each adjustment period.

Hard Money Loan: This is the least popular type of loan for primary residences. A hard money loan is generally used for a short duration of time. It has a lower origination fee, time to close, and it's easier to secure. However, the interest rates are much higher. This type of loan is popular for homes that a traditional mortgage company might stay away from, such as a fixer upper.

Mortgage Points

If you have a hard time coming to terms with a high interest rate, you can spend money to reduce your interest rate by a certain amount. A single mortgage point is equal to 1% of the total mortgage amount and generally lowers your interest rate by 0.25%. For example, you can spend $3,000 to reduce the interest rate on your $300k mortgage by 0.25%. You may wonder whether it's worth it. As usual, it comes down to a math exercise. Let's assume a 7% interest rate on the abovementioned parameters:

- How much will it save you monthly?
  - For this scenario, the original mortgage is $1,996/month for just the principal and interest. After applying $3,000 to lower the interest rate by 0.25%, the monthly payment is $1,946, representing a decrease of $50/month.
- How long do you have to hold the house before you break even?
  - Not taking into account inflation and the time value of money, it would take 60 payments or 5 years to recover the original $3,000 cost.
- How long does it really take to break even?
  - If you take into account inflation of 3%, then you will find that your $50/month has less buying power over the years after you apply your $3,000 in mortgage points. Therefore, if you run a net present value (NPV) calculation, you will find the breakeven point to be between 5 and 6 years. See Section "Financial Formulas" in the appendix for the NPV calculation.
  - If you take into account the opportunity cost of investing your money into your retirement accounts, your discount rate becomes 8%. Rerunning the NPV calculation, you will find the breakeven point to be just shy of 7 years.

Mortgage points are paid at the close of the home along with your down payment, escrow, title fees, and so on. Mortgage points can sometimes add a hefty sum to your closing costs and may not be worth it for you at the time. Mortgage points are considered to be prepaid interest; therefore, money spent on points is also tax deductible for the year that you closed on the house. For example, if you spend $6,000 on mortgage points and pay $10,000 in interest in the year that you purchased the home, you are eligible to deduct $16,000 off your taxes if you itemize.

You can also use points to settle on a slightly higher interest rate in exchange for lower closing costs, known as a lender credit. In the abovementioned scenario, rather than paying $3,000, your closing costs are lowered by $3,000, but you are on the hook for an extra $50/month for the life of the loan. If you plan on holding the home for a short period of time and are short on closing cash, it may be mathematically advantageous to do this. As usual, it is imperative to perform the calculations to see when the breakeven point occurs!

How Much House Can You Afford?

The rule of thumb is to buy a house that is three to four times your annual gross income and to ensure that the total mortgage, including maintenance and utilities, does not exceed 33% of your gross income (approximately 25% for the mortgage, 5% for utilities, and 3% for maintenance). There are many factors that play into this, such as your interest rate, local property taxes, HOA (homeowners association) costs, the age of the home that will influence maintenance costs, and your own job security. You need to make several key calculations when budgeting to purchase a home:

- Monthly principal and interest payment
  - This calculation is fairly straightforward as it is simply based on the loan amount and interest rate. The calculation can be done in any online mortgage calculator.[46]
- Property tax (as a percentage of the county assessed home value)
  - Annual property tax is calculated by taking the county assessed value of your home and subtracting qualified deductions, then multiplying by the state property tax rate. Note that in addition to the state property tax rate, there may be additional local taxes that are intended to fund certain township items.
- Approximate homeowners insurance
  - The best way to get a homeowners insurance range is to get a quote. The cost of insurance varies greatly from area to area since it takes into consideration the type of coverage and deductible, age of home, value of land versus home, security system, safety of surrounding neighborhood, likelihood of natural disaster, and other local data. A good preliminary estimate to use is about 0.2% to 0.4% of the home value per year.

- HOA fee
  - This ranges from zero to several hundred dollars per month or even over a thousand dollars a month for super luxury apartments. In general, single-family homes have low HOAs, townhomes have mid-priced HOAs, and condos have relatively high HOA fees. It's important to understand the conditions of the HOA that include visitor and renting rules, pet rules, and other stipulations. Additionally, you should understand what they cover for you in terms of maintenance and upkeep. They can sometimes be more efficient than doing it yourself, especially if you are not interested in the traditional property maintenance responsibilities of the typical homeowner.
- Estimated maintenance on the home
  - This is typically 1% to 2% of the home's value annually. For older homes, you may have to budget 2%, and for newer homes 1%. If the home is coming up on a major maintenance milestone (roof, HVAC overhaul, etc.), you may have to factor that into your purchase price and remaining cash reserve as there is a chance that it needs to be done immediately or within the first year of ownership. A good inspection performed prior to purchasing the home can uncover expected maintenance items you might need to perform in your ownership.
- Utilities
  - Many folks are surprised by how much utilities cost for home versus apartments. This stems from several different factors. Firstly, homes tend to be larger than apartments, which will require a larger amount of energy to heat and cool. Secondly, homes tend not to be clustered together and not share walls, which increases exposure to elements.

Setting a budget for a home isn't necessarily as straightforward as adding up all of the items and making sure they land within a certain percentage of your monthly payment. There are many other factors you should consider. For example, if you plan on staying in the home for a very long time, you may opt to purchase a slightly larger home that may fit your future family. The higher mortgage upfront could save you money in transactional costs involved in upgrading to a larger home, as long as the upgrade was bound to happen sooner rather than later. The mortgage on your home will increase slightly as property value and home insurance increase, but it will likely not outpace your rising income, especially if you are a young professional. While it may not make sense on paper to purchase a home that is "too expensive" now, it may benefit you in the future if you decide to stay for an extended period of time! Keep in mind that this book's definition of "too expensive" is not the same as the bank's definition of "too expensive," which is likely way more than what you can comfortably afford. It is also wise to pad your homeownership cost by about 10% to accommodate any surprise monthly expenses or the increased monthly costs throughout the first few years of ownership. It is always a good idea to leave some breathing room in your budget as raises in your job are not guaranteed and the increased costs in homeownership can fluctuate sporadically. For example, recently homes in the southern United States in hurricane-prone areas have been receiving updates to their homeowners insurance policies that have increased the cost of insurance to anywhere from 50% to 100% due to increased risk of natural disaster. Jumps didn't happen gradually over several years, but all at once.

How Much *Should* I Put Down?

Traditionalists will say that you have to put at least 20% down on a home. There are a myriad of good reasons for this, particularly in a high-interest-rate market. However, the mathematics of this can get complicated. Putting less than 20% down will result in a higher mortgage payment due to a larger loan, and the inclusion of PMI to your monthly payment. You may be thinking, "Why would anyone put less than 20% down!?" In fact, there are plenty of reasons why someone might put a small down payment on a home, including getting into the market earlier, taking advantage of a low interest rate, maintaining a larger emergency fund, or using the cash in another investment that may return more than the mortgage interest rate. Even if none of the abovementioned pertains to you, let's look at a very interesting analysis that sheds some light as to why the line between 5% and 20% down is so blurred.

It's January 2025 and you're finally ready to begin saving for a house. Your HHI is $150k/year, which enables you to save about $20k/year. Your budget is a house that is, in today's dollars, $500k. Let's assume the following parameters: 7% mortgage interest rate and 3% annual home value appreciation.[47]

Scenario A: You want to put down 20% for your home. This would require a $100k down payment and about $10k in closing costs, so approximately $110k total. This takes 5.5 years to save for. In those 5.5 years, the home actually appreciated to $588k, which means it will actually take 6.5 to 7 years to save up the down payment of $132k. Your mortgage payment (principal and interest only), beginning in 2032, will be $3,130/month and you will start with a 0.8 LTV ratio ($122k in equity, $488k mortgage) with no PMI.

Scenario B: You plan on putting down 5% on the home, which would require approximately $25k and about $10k in closing costs for a total of $35k. This takes around 2 years to save up. The home has appreciated to $530k, which means it would take closer to $36.5k to close, which is still achievable in 2 years. At the 2-year mark, you purchase the home. Your mortgage payment will be $3,350/month and your PMI is $100/month, bringing your total monthly payment to $3,450. You begin at a 0.95 LTV ratio at Year 2. By Year 7, when Scenario A folks are able to buy, your home has appreciated from $530k to $588k. During this time, you have accumulated $137.4k in equity, which is a result of both home appreciation ($58k) and loan paydown ($79.4k including down payment). Your LTV is now 0.766 and your PMI is now able to be taken off. In this time, you have spent $8,400 on PMI, but as we can see, the appreciation and equity built in the house offset the PMI amount.

Discussion: We can see that in both scenarios, the outcomes in year 2032 are fiscally similar. Note that in the 4 years that Scenario A used to save for the full 20% down payment and Scenario B was able to re-allocate the $20k/year to other financial goals while Scenario A had to continue paying both rent *and* saving up for the home (assuming that the rental and home are comparable costs). $20k over 5 years is $100k, which the $200/month difference in mortgage will never make up (it will take 500 months to make that amount up). Scenario B will come out ahead financially in the end, and they will finish their mortgage 5 years earlier.

You may be thinking about how the 3% home appreciation assumption greatly sways the math in Scenario B's favor. Let's do the same case study with a 0% home appreciation rate.

Scenario C: You want to put down 20% for your home. This would require a $100k down payment and about $10k in closing costs, so approximately $110k to close. This takes 5.5 years to save for. Your mortgage payment, beginning in 2031, will be $2,661/month and you will start with a 0.8 LTV ratio ($100k in equity) with no PMI.

Scenario D: You plan on putting down 5% on the home, which would require approximately $25k and about $10k in closing costs for a total of $35k. At the 2-year mark, you purchase the home. Your mortgage payment will be $3,160/month and your PMI is $100/month, bringing your total monthly payment to $3,260. In 2027, you begin at a 0.95 LTV ratio. By 2031, when Scenario A folks are able to buy, you have accumulated $60.3k in equity from loan paydown. Your LTV is now 0.88 and your PMI can be taken off in 5 years. The total amount paid to PMI is approximately $13.2k. In this time, you were able to save an extra $60k, minus the extra $21.6k spent in mortgage payments. You have about $40k liquid cash to utilize but a substantially higher mortgage payment.

Discussion: It is extremely rare to see zero home appreciation[48] in a 5-year window in the U.S. history. However, that doesn't mean that it is impossible. The numbers in both scenarios are a lot closer than one might think. Additionally, a $100/month PMI payment should not be the deciding factor when purchasing a $500k home, since utilities and maintenance expenses can vary far more than $100/month.

Disclaimer: I am not suggesting that you put down as little as possible. Rather, I am stating that if you do not have the funds to put 20% down but you meet the conservative financial requirements laid out in this text for homebuying, then putting less than 20% down and paying PMI is not the end of the world and isn't that much more expensive than putting 20% down. Nevertheless, if you have the cash available, then the best course of action is usually to use it for the down payment. A compromise that you can make is to put down 5%, but aggressively save the next 15% in a HYSA, then recast the mortgage once you have enough saved up to lower your monthly payment. This will place you at the 0.8 LTV and could enable you to get your PMI removed.

Ultimately, it is important to consider your personal situation and needs. If you are just buying a house for the sake of buying a house, it is worth another look to understand your optimal timing. However, if you are emotionally, logistically, and financially ready to purchase a house, it may be better to do it sooner rather than later. As discussed, purchasing a home is not only about the numbers, but it is also about your personal life, personal preferences, desire for flexibility, and so on. Naturally, market upsets may skew these numbers; however, the data show that the market is in your favor in general!

Recasting Versus Refinance Versus HELOC Versus Home Equity Loan

Your mortgage is some of the cheapest money you'll borrow in your life, even when rates are relatively high! The reason for this is that your mortgage is backed by your home, which does not generally swing much in value. It may seem like a great idea to pay off your 7% mortgage over investing into the market, but there is a caveat: The money is not liquid. The equity in your home is "trapped," and it costs money to turn that equity into cash. On the other hand, a stock or index fund investment can be liquidated with relative ease. While you should not be treating your home equity like a piggy bank, it is important to understand how to tap into your home equity in the event that you need it, such as for a large home renovation. In this section, we will discuss how to add or remove equity into your home.

Recasting a Mortgage

Suppose you use one of the discussed scenarios: You saved up 20% down payment but only put 5% down on your home just in case you came upon some unexpected maintenance for the home. After you bought the home, you realized you don't need that money in liquid cash, and you're stuck paying PMI and a super high mortgage! Luckily, most lenders offer an option to recast. Typically, paying a large lump sum to your mortgage will allow your mortgage to end earlier since your principal will decrease and, in turn, your interest paid over the life of the loan will decrease.

Instead, you may want the loan term to remain the same but have your monthly payment decrease. In this case, you would use the recast option. You are able to make a lump sum payment and then have your monthly payment adjusted to reflect the new principal amount and keep the loan duration. This option typically does not cost any money or change your interest rate, but it can save you money throughout the life of the loan by hacking away at loan principal, thereby reducing interest paid annually.

Refinancing a Loan

If you have the opportunity to decrease your interest rate by 0.5% or more, then you might want to consider refinancing. When you refinance a mortgage, it will cost money to underwrite the loan. Typically, it will cost around 2% to 6% of the loan amount, and it takes around 1 to 2 years to break even. When refinancing, you have the option to take out equity from your home—this is known as a cash-out refinance. To do this, you take out a new loan that is larger than what you need to cover the existing loan (as long as the new loan does not exceed the LTV ratio limit set by your lender). After you pay off the existing loan, you take the remaining cash and use it for other things. Taking out cash for luxury purchases is a bad idea, but taking out cash for large home renovations or additional investments such as purchasing another property MIGHT be a good idea if the interest rates are in your favor (beware of overleveraging).

Home Equity Line of Credit (HELOC)

Perhaps you purchased your home at a very low interest rate and refinancing is not in the cards for you. You can open a HELOC, which is a variable interest loan that you can use from month to month. It's essentially a credit card backed by your home. It costs a small amount of money to open this line of credit, but it is a good tool to use if you need cash at a lower-than-traditional-credit-card interest rate. Note that there are minimum requirements to open a HELOC, which include credit scores, DTI ratio limits, and minimum home equity. Most HELOC lenders will allow you to borrow 80% to 85% of your built equity.

Home Equity Loan (HEL)

Perhaps the idea of the variable interest rate scares you and you only need a single loan. You can take out a HEL, which is a fixed-interest loan that is backed by your home value. While it's not as flexible as the credit card–like HELOC, it's fixed interest and has fixed repayment amounts every month.

Conclusion

The methods discussed should only be used in the right conditions. Many people regularly take out cash or equity from their primary residence and end up paying off their mortgage late into retirement. Your home is not a piggy bank. It is important to run the numbers on each option to determine which is best for your situation. For costly home improvements, many contracting companies offer low-interest financing. Most importantly, any loans (HELOC or HEL) taken using your home as collateral means that if you cannot repay the loan, the bank will foreclose on your home. In a typical bankruptcy scenario, your primary residence is immune to relief. On the contrary, HELOCs and HELs are not immune and you must foreclose or sell the home to rid yourself of that debt in the event of inability to repay.

The Cost of Capital

A lot of people think of interest paid as a flat amount. If you buy a house, you will generally pay the same total monthly principal and interest over time (although your balance between principal and interest will shift in your favor as the loan gets paid down). In this section, we will discuss the true "cost" of borrowing money.

Consider the following mortgage: $300k house, $240k loan, 30 year, 6% interest. Your monthly loan payment will be $1,439, which is $519k over the life of the loan—over double the amount of your original mortgage! Your total interest over the life of the loan is $278k, but recall that money in the future is worth less than money today. In other words, every dollar in interest you pay in the future is worth less than a dollar in interest today. The fact that you don't have to pay June 2040's interest payment today is fantastic and definitely worth something! How much is it worth, exactly? As a conservative estimate, you can use the inflation rate of 2.5% and discount all of your interest payments back to today's dollars for a true sense of how much your mortgage will cost. The NPV of this interest amount at a 2.5% discount rate is $213k, which is a much more reasonable number! This is the actual cost, in today's dollars, of borrowing this money. It really helps put large loans into a more manageable perspective!

Another way to look at it is using the opportunity cost concept, which takes into account not only your interest payment but also your entire principal and interest payment! Instead of purchasing your property in cash, you are able to utilize your cash for something else and take out a mortgage for your home. Luckily, you don't have to pay the 2040 mortgage payment until 2040, and the payment will be identical to what it is today. However, due to inflation, that purchasing power will be lower relative to what it is today, kind of like how your boomer grandparents' mortgage was probably $4 and a stick of gum. The NPV with 2.5% is only $358k in today's dollars. This represents the actual cost of your purchase in today's dollars. If your interest rate is below the average rate of inflation, you actually make money by borrowing this money and the bank loses money. Part of the COVID economy stimulation was the Federal Reserve lowering interest rates to 0%, which made mortgages ultra-affordable. People were receiving 2% interest loans! As inflation and interest rates rose post-pandemic, the fortunate people who took out ultra-low-interest mortgages are actually making money on the deal.

In the short run, the market and inflation don't follow these generalizations due to speculative fluctuations. If you plan on holding your home for a relatively short period of time, these calculations don't necessarily hold up. The point of this exercise is to incorporate the ideas of opportunity cost, inflation, interest, discounted cash flow analysis, and NPV, all into a single comprehensive topic so that you can truly understand the utility of money!

The Homebuying Timeline

The homebuying process varies from deal to deal, but it ultimately boils down to a few key chunks of time. Disclaimer: I am not a licensed real estate agent, but I asked my realtor as many questions as I possibly could in order to understand the why, what, and how of each step in the process and in order to navigate it with as little risk as possible. You should do the same with your realtor.

There are a lot of steps in this process, and while we will not cover all of the permutations of steps that you will encounter, we will discuss some details in the traditional order. Even just having a general sense of the nuances involved at each step will help you make a more informed decision and strategize accordingly.

Identify Your Personal Needs

Nobody knows what you need more than you! Make sure you lay out the basics of what you want, including how many bedrooms and bathrooms, general location, school system, square footage range, garage space, yard space, and more. Then, make sure you list the details including layout preferences (bed/bath orientations, living room and kitchen layout, walk-in pantry, etc.), age of home, utility types like tankless versus tank water heater, and dual-zone versus single-zone AC units. Then, divide your list into must-haves and nice-to-haves. The more detailed you make this list, the easier it will be to identify homes that check all your boxes!

Screening

You do not need a realtor at this stage. At this point, you can go onto any popular real estate site and search for homes that meet your criteria. Popular sites are Zillow, Realtor.com, and HAR. Be sure to save your searches and turn notifications on so you receive e-mails when a house pops up that fits your criteria. The purpose of this stage is to get your creative juices flowing. Maybe what you envisioned to be your ideal house is not what you actually want! More importantly, you need to make sure that the house you envision exists and is within your budget. You don't want to ask your realtor to find you a 5,000 square foot house in Los Angeles for $400k!

Prequalification

Before you finalize your budget, you need to ensure that a bank will actually lend you the amount that you are looking to borrow. Getting a prequalification counts as a soft credit pull. Typically, this value is simply based on your credit score, income, and current debts. Your bank will use that information to estimate how much they are willing to lend to you. The amount varies greatly, but it is typically between 3× and 5× your annual gross income, pending your current DTI. Note that just because a lender *prequalifies* you for an amount doesn't mean that you will get *approval* for that amount. Also note that you will likely get prequalified for way more house than will be comfortable for you in the long run. Homebuying is a very emotional decision, and you may be tempted to increase your budget if you find your dream home. Stick to your budget and do not let your emotions override it.

Get a Realtor

A good realtor is worth their weight in gold. They are your representative for navigating deals, and they are largely responsible for providing you with viable options to choose from. Your realtor usually handles all of the communications with the seller's agent. A professional realtor has access to the multiple listing service (MLS), which has all listings, including those that may not be available to the public. Most importantly, a good realtor will have a deep understanding of the local market and state laws. Finding a good realtor is one of the most important steps in the homebuying process. They can save you a tremendous amount of headache and money. On the other hand, do not be afraid to leave a bad realtor. You don't owe them anything.

Provide the Realtor with Your Requirements

In order for your realtor to best serve you, you must provide a list of the requirements for your new home. These can be as broad and specific as you'd like, but the more info you provide, the less time you'll waste on properties that don't match what you're looking for! Understand that a more detailed set of criteria will make the search process produce less results but with greater likelihood of success! Here is a list of common preferences you should submit to your realtor:

- Budget range
- Type of home (apartment/condo, townhome, single-family home, multifamily, etc.)

- General area or neighborhood
- HOA existence and/or cost
- Interior square footage (a range will usually suffice)
- Garage versus no garage
- Number of bedrooms and bathrooms (and sizes if there is a preference)
- Exterior amenities (deck, yard, driveway, garden, trees, fences, etc.)
- Internal layout (central vs. partitioned, two large floors vs. three smaller floors, ceiling height)
- Types of materials (flooring, counters, bathroom tiles, etc.)
- Internal amenities (stainless steel appliances, wine fridge or bar, kitchen island, countertop material, flooring selection and color, wall colors, bathroom and shower styles, walk-in closet configuration)
- Foundation style (slab vs. pier and beam)
- Other amenities and details (light fixtures, smart features, window size and placement, number and orientation of closets)

It seems like a very exhaustive list, but the more detail you give your realtor, the easier it will be to say no to a property and move onto the next one and the easier it will be to know when you've found a property that checks all your boxes!

Get Pre-Approval

The preapproval process is complicated and tiresome. Your lender will want every detail of your financial situation in order to verify that you are able to take on the mortgage. Here is list of *some* of the things that they will want:

- Banking statements from all accounts, including investments (at least 2 months for each account)
- Full credit report
- Proof of employment and date of hire, in addition to explanations for employment gaps

- Pay stubs from current and past jobs
- Tax forms from years back to support asset list
- Signed letters explaining unusual activity (which may be simply transferring money from one account to another)

This is not an exhaustive list, and the level of detail may vary from lender to lender. In general, you want to get this list together ASAP and send it over to the lender so they can cross-check with your credit report and make sure you're good to go.

Tour!

Go on as many tours as you can! Once you begin touring homes, you might make modifications to your preferences list upon physically stepping into various homes. Note that you do not need realtor representation for open houses while you do need your realtor to be with you for private tours. Typically, it is ill-advised to tour with the selling agent as they don't have your best interests at heart. Your interests should be your own realtor's top priority, so tour with them whenever possible. Once you schedule a tour with a house that is for sale, your realtor should send over any documentation from the MLS about the house including photos, details about the house, and comps (comparisons) to nearby homes that have been recently sold.

Offer: Place an Offer on a Place That You Like

Although you are able to submit an offer to a home without touring, it is highly recommended that you at least walk through a place before submitting an offer. An offer consists of more than just the purchase price. It can have contingencies, timeline stipulations, inspection waivers, and more. While we will chat about some of the knobs you can adjust in your offer, the process of how to navigate this will not be discussed in depth here and is best left to a good realtor to help you.

Counteroffer: Receive a Counteroffer from the Seller

This part is self-explanatory. You may receive a counteroffer from the sellers or straight-up rejection. It's just part of the process.

Negotiate: Repeat the Previous Two Steps Until You Reach an Agreement

You should have an open discussion with your agent as to how to navigate an offer after a tour. The sellers may receive several offers and will consider the best one. They may not always pick the highest numerical offer. For example, a house is listed at $500k. A conventional buyer with 30% down may offer $495k while an FHA buyer with 3.5% down may offer $505k. Even though the FHA offer is $10k more, there is a higher likelihood of the FHA loan not being approved versus a conventional loan, and the sellers may choose the conventional loan to avoid the home sitting on the market for too long. Here are some examples of knobs you can adjust when making an offer:

- Waive inspections (ill-advised, but speeds up the process and makes it less likely that you'll back out of the deal due to finding something wrong with the house).
- Ask seller to pay closing costs—This sounds like a "why would anyone agree to that" type deal, but it has been done in cooler markets. There have also been methods to offer the seller say $10k more for a home in exchange for a $9k credit toward closing costs. This will enable you to come to close with less cash. This may be beneficial in a low-interest environment. Note that the $1k difference is because the seller will have to pay realtor fees and potentially even taxes on the extra $10k.
- Offer more option money—Option money is nonrefundable money usually of around a few hundred dollars that buys you time to complete inspections and due diligence. Higher option money demonstrates your commitment to the deal.
- Longer or shorter option period—The option period is typically 7 to 14 days that you can use to have all inspections performed on the house. During this period, you are able to back out of the deal and only sacrifice your option money.
- Waive financing addendum—The financing addendum allows you to back out of the deal without penalty (except option money) if you are not approved for your mortgage. If you waive this and your lender doesn't approve your financing, you are out your earnest money.

- Include or not include appliances—This is self-explanatory, but it is typical not to include appliances. You may request that appliances to be included. They can get very expensive, so it's a good tactic to try.

Option Money

Once the seller agrees and accepts your offer, you have X days (as detailed by the contract) to provide option money, which begins the option period. The option period is the time in which you perform all of your inspections and due diligence on the home.

Option/Inspection Period

As mentioned, during the option period, you perform all your inspections. In addition to a standard overall home inspection, it is recommended that you have other related inspections for your area. Examples include termite/pest inspections, stucco inspections, foundation/structural inspections, plumbing/electrical inspections, and so on. While it may be eye-watering to spend hundreds of dollars on each inspection, it will buy you peace of mind before submitting your earnest money. Any of the mentioned issues may cost thousands of dollars if major problems arise. Note that while the seller is legally required to disclose any existing problems with the house, that doesn't always happen or they may not know themselves. It is always a good idea to check with a third party before proceeding. Just chalk this up to the cost of doing business.

During this period, you may also ask for seller concession, which is money back from the seller toward closing costs for a variety of reasons. For example, during the inspections you find some water damage in the sheetrock that will cost $1,000 to repair. You really love the house and you don't want to back out. You can simply ask the seller for a $1,000 concession due to the unexpected damage found. The sellers can agree or disagree, and it will be your decision to back out of the deal by the end of the option period and forfeit your option money.

Earnest Money Deposit

At or before the end of the option period, you can either back out of the deal or provide earnest money simultaneously with signing the contract. There may be a variety of reasons that you back out of a deal, such as finding another place that you like better, the inspections coming back less-than-stellar, or your financing being rejected. An earnest money deposit is 1% to 10% of the agreed-upon purchase price of the home, typically 1%. Your earnest money is refundable pending the terms of the agreed-upon contract. In some markets, earnest money is used in place of option money, but it retains refundability. Your realtor will know the specifics of how to navigate the deal since they should understand the local market and laws. Your earnest money will count toward cash to close when the deal gets finalized.

Contract Finalization

You will now finalize the contract by determining a closing date, and the bank will now work toward loan finalization. The closing date estimation varies from bank to bank, but is typically 3 to 5 weeks after contract finalization and will depend on how quickly you can finalize financing and, hence, the point about negotiability. A month is approximately the industry standard.

Loan Finalization

Even if you are already preapproved for your loan, you still need to work with your bank to get final approval and submit all documents requested by them. They may ask for additional clarification on multiple items, so be prepared to answer questions.

Final Walkthrough

A few days before you close (sometimes it's the day of close), you will do a final walkthrough of the home with your realtor. This is to ensure that the sellers have not changed anything before moving out. Once you approve of the final walkthrough, you are ready to close!

Close on the House!

Sometimes you meet with everyone at the house itself, and sometimes you go into the title company office, sign a bunch of papers, and get handed the deed and other associated paperwork. Congratulations, you're a homeowner!

CHAPTER 11

Financial Psychology

In lieu of the plethora of detail presented in this book, I can summarize *how to be successful with your finances* on a single sheet of paper,[49] akin to Warren Buffet's punch-card strategy. The key takeaways from each chapter can be easily distilled into a few sentences or even a diagram. In fact, you could have stopped reading after "The Flow of Personal Finance" and you would have been more financially knowledgeable than many young professionals. Above all, the most challenging thing to overcome in your journey is your own psychology.

In the process of writing this book, I have spoken to dozens of people regarding their financial situations. They were all in various stages of their journeys and had varying assets and incomes. I generally give people the same mathematically optimal advice as is given in this book, but one common denominator among people is that everyone has a unique view of money that has impacted their ability or desire to follow the optimal path. One person might be overly risk tolerant while another might be overly risk averse. One person might want to keep a higher than recommended emergency fund due to having a poor medical history while another might want a small emergency fund because they have a lot of passive income that can sustain their modest lifestyle. It is clear that knowing what to do is very different than doing that thing. Nonetheless, in all the conversations I have had with people, the most important thing I work to instill upon them is all the tools they have at their disposal and how using them differently might impact their bottom line.

The point of this discussion, and this book in general, is not to encourage you to think in a certain way or to have a certain attitude toward money. Rather, the objective is to help you become aware that your financial psychology and emotional relationship with money will have a far greater impact than you might think, and using math to understand exactly how it impacts your financial decisions is imperative. There is no one right way of looking at money, but you must understand the implications of your choices, for better or worse.

CHAPTER 12

Conclusion

Now that you have finished this book, I hope that you have developed not only a general understanding of personal finance but also an appreciation for tools at your disposal to achieve your definition of financial success. The tools, however, are not limited to those presented in this book, so be sure to continue learning. This will take years, perhaps your entire life—and your emotional relationship with money will continue to develop and mature as you earn more money, introduce greater expenses, ride through market fluctuations, and develop a better understanding of what you want out of life. Remember that money is a tool for you to be able to live life the way that you want to live it.

Do not worry if you are not perfectly optimized now or if you have errors to fix. Every day, month, or year, you can move closer to your optimal financial state and learn from your mistakes. Mistakes are bound to happen, and nothing ever goes completely as planned. That's what makes life interesting!

If you are still overwhelmed, don't worry! It takes a long time to learn and internalize something as complex as personal finance. Like a foreign language, it takes practice, experience, and exposure to become fluent. There is an abundance of other personal finance books and resources that you could use to enhance your understanding. The concepts discussed in this book will overlap with those in other books of this era, but remember: The most important things about personal finance are that you understand (1) the tools at your disposal, (2) that how you use those tools will influence your financial future, and (3) that your psychological and emotional relationship with money is paramount. There isn't a single best way to achieve financial freedom. Take bits of pieces of what you learn from books like these, people who are successful, and your own curiosity to build a system that works for you and will follow forever. Lastly, it will take time—lots of it. Be patient. If there was an easy way to get rich quick (there isn't), then everybody would be rich.

I wish you the best in your personal finance journey and hope that you feel prepared to take the first steps in bringing yourself to financial freedom! I also hope you have developed a genuine interest in personal finance. Understanding the beast makes it so much less of a chore, and, when it's not a chore, you are more likely to continue with it in the long run!

Appendix

The 15% Rule for Retirement Calculations

Your goal for retirement is to save up 25× your expenses so you can draw down 4% of it each year. For simplicity, let's say your expenses in retirement are equal to your current salary. This is an ultra-conservative approach, since, in reality, you only need 25× of your expenses, which will be your current salary minus your savings. It is much easier to achieve 25× your expenses versus 25× of your salary. Nonetheless, we use the following equation to calculate investment growth:

$$FV = \sum_{n=0}^{N} P(1+r)^n$$

Where P = annual contribution, r = annual growth rate (assume 7%), and N is number of years until retirement. This is a partial sum of a geometric series:

$$FV = \frac{P\left(1-(1+r)^N\right)}{1-(1+r)} \Rightarrow \frac{P\left(1-(1+r)^N\right)}{-r} \Rightarrow \frac{P\left(1-1.07^N\right)}{-0.07}$$

Our goal is for this sum to be approximately 25× of your current annual salary, 's':

$$\frac{P\left(1-1.07^N\right)}{-0.07} = 25s$$

The relationship between P and s is that the annual contribution (P) is your savings rate (R) times your salary (s):

$$P = Rs$$

Substituting into the earlier equation gives

$$\frac{Rs\left(1-1.07^{N}\right)}{-0.07} = 25s \Rightarrow \frac{R\left(1-1.07^{N}\right)}{-0.07} = 25$$

Solving for R gives

$$R(N) = \frac{25(-0.07)}{1-1.07^{N}} \Rightarrow R(N) = \frac{1.75}{1.07^{N}-1}$$

This is an elegant demonstration of the savings rate required for the number of years until retirement. For $N = 39$ years (median new college graduate and retiree are 23 and 62, respectively), $R(39) = 0.1347$, or 13.5%.

Figure A.1 shows the curve of $R(N)$ with the number of years until retirement on the x-axis and the savings rate as a decimal on the y-axis. The golden ratio of 10% to 20% assumes that you will work for somewhere between 35 and 45 years. If you wish to retire early, you can save as much as 60% of your income!

Required Savings Rate as a Function of Working Years

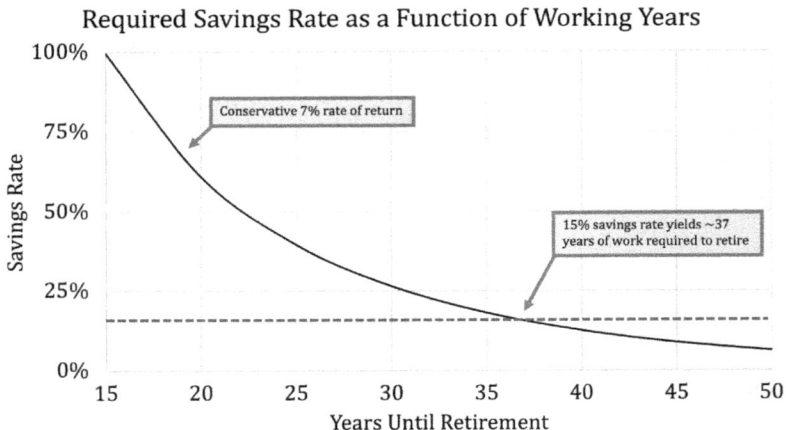

Figure A.1 Required savings rate as a function of working years

Note that the biggest assumption here is that your rate of return is going to be a constant 7% and that your future expenses will match your current salary. This does not account for potentially paying off your home before retiring, getting salary increases throughout your career, or lifestyle inflation as you grow older. The 15% rule is a ballpark estimate that is small enough not to make or break your budget, but large enough to help you get into the habit of saving and investing your money for your future! (Figure A.2).

Required Savings Rate as a Function of Working Years

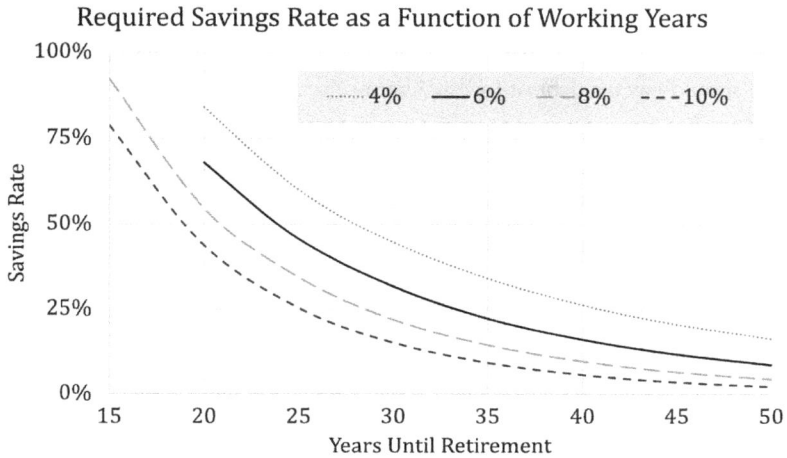

Figure A.2 *Required savings rate as a function of working years (multiple growth rates)*

A more comprehensive analysis utilizes various rates of return that might occur over the next 60+ years. The results are shown in Table A.1:

Table A.1 *Required savings rate table based on 4% withdrawal rate*

Years Until Retirement	Annual Growth Rate (in %)			
	4	6	8	10
15			92	79
20	84	68	55	44
25	60	46	34	25
30	45	32	22	15
35	34	22	15	9
40	26	16	10	6
45	21	12	6	3
50	16	9	4	2

Note: Savings rates above 90% have been removed. In reality, the bottom rows and rightmost column will not be a likely scenario. People who experience high rates of return are unlikely to work for 50+ years. The average years of work is somewhere in the 35 to 40-year range, as noted in bold. Using an average rate of return around 7%, it is evident where the 15% rule came from. More conservative folks may choose to use 20%, and people who plan on working longer may use 10%.

Why Is 5% the Threshold for Paying Off Debt Versus Investing

The threshold for investing versus paying off debt isn't exactly 5%; it's somewhere between 4% and 6% depending on your personal risk tolerance and other factors such as whether the loan interest is tax deductible. This example will go through some considerations to help you decide whether you should pay off debt or invest. Assumptions:

- Your marginal overall tax rate on invested income is 25%.
- Your interest paid on the loan is nondeductible.
- Rate of return is 5.625% based on: 10% annual market return over past 30 years, minus 2.5% for inflation, then reduced by 25% for tax.
- You take out a 10-year loan for $10,000.

Let's say that for both situations, you have $200/month cash either to put toward your loan or invest. Over a 10-year period, the total amount is $24,000. Subtracting the original $10,000 loan, your final net worth is $14,000.

Situation A: Prioritize investing with a low-interest loan
Your loan interest rate is 4%, making the monthly payment $101.25. Over the life of the loan, you will have paid $12,149.42 in total. On the investment side, you invest the remaining $98.75 per month, compounding at 5.625%. At the end of the 10 years, you will have $15,738.64.
Situation B: Prioritize loan repayment with a low-interest loan
Same as Situation A, but instead of investing, you use your entire monthly contribution of $200 toward debt. It takes you 4 years and 7 months to pay off the loan entirely, which leaves 5 years and 5 months to invest. Using the same abovementioned return, but only investing for 5 years and 5 months, you will have $15,108.40 at the end of the period.

Situation A Versus Situation B Discussion: The results are surprisingly similar; investing early only barely edges out paying off debt early. The benefit is the liquidity of your investment throughout the entire loan period. For some people a difference of $600 over 10 years is a small price to pay.

Situation C: Prioritize investing with a higher interest loan

Your loan interest rate is 6%, making your monthly payment $111.02. Over the life of the loan, you will have paid $13,322.46 in total. On the investment side, you invest $88.98, compounding at 5.625%. At the end of the 10 years, you will have $14,181.51 in investments.

Situation D: Prioritize loan repayment with a higher interest rate

You initially use your entire monthly contribution of $200 toward debt. It takes you 4 years and 10 months to pay off the loan entirely, which leaves 5 years and 2 months to invest. Using the same abovementioned return, but investing for only 5 years and 2 months, you will have $14,308.55 at the end of the period.

Situation C Versus Situation D Discussion: The results again are surprisingly similar, with paying off debt early slightly edging out investing early. We can see that the breakeven point is somewhere between 4% and 6% interest. The investment rate of return is also highly subjective. It is worthwhile to perform these kinds of calculations on your own scenarios to see which is mathematically optimal.

Note: In addition to paying off relatively low-interest debt early resulting in a relatively small difference in total money spent, when doing so, you will have extremely low liquidity. Therefore, if cash is needed at some point in the future, that money is inaccessible. Money contributed toward a single large loan does not change your DTI ratio or change your baseline monthly expenses. Even money placed into home equity must be extracted via a costly mortgage refinance, a HELOC, or home equity loan.

Financial One-Pager (Figure A.3)

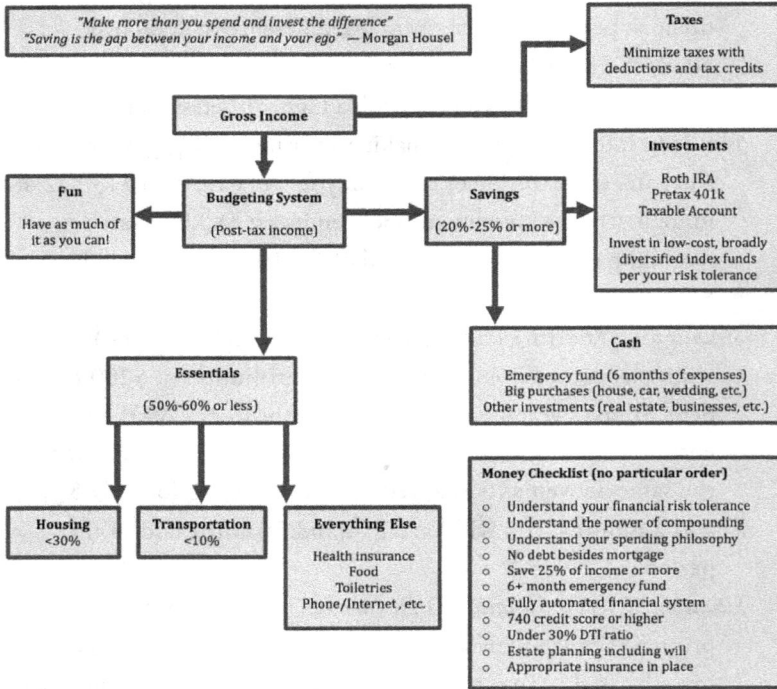

Figure A.3 *Personal finance one-pager*

Financial Formulas

n = number of periods	t = time (in years)	r = rate of return
i = interest rate	P = principal balance (of loan)	V = value
C = contribution per period	c = change as a percent	

$$\text{Percent of a number} = \frac{\text{Part}}{\text{Whole}} \cdot 100\%$$

$$\text{Percent change}: c = \frac{\text{New} - \text{Old}}{\text{Old}} \cdot 100\%$$

Simple growth of a single contribution: [FV] = $P + Prt \Rightarrow$ [FV] = $P(1 + rt)$

The average rate of return (ROR) requires information about the starting and ending value as well as the number of years that this return has occurred.

$$\text{Average ROR} : r = \left(\frac{c}{100}\right)^{\frac{1}{t}}$$

A quick and dirty way to approximate the number of years needed to double your money at any interest rate is the Rule of 72:

$$t = \frac{72}{r}$$

The precise method to calculate the future value of a current investment with a specified annual growth rate over a period of time is the Future Value equation.

$$\text{Annual compound growth: [FV]} = \text{[PV]} \cdot (1 + r)^t$$

If your growth is compounded more frequently than annually, then you may implement n, the number of compounding periods (monthly is $n = 12$, weekly is $n = 52$, etc.)

$$\text{Future Value} : \left[FV\right] = \left[PV\right] \cdot \left(1 + \frac{r}{n}\right)^{nt}$$

Solving for [PV] allows you to calculate the present value of an investment if you know the future value. This is useful when trying to set goals of what you need now to prepare for your future.

$$\text{Present Value} : \left[PV\right] = \frac{\left[FV\right]}{\left(1 + \dfrac{r}{n}\right)^{nt}}$$

In reality, you would contribute consistently to an account that will grow over time. The equation used to calculate the final value of a consistent annual contribution is:

$$[\text{FV}] = \sum_{k=1}^{t} \left[C(1+r)^{k-1} \right] \Rightarrow [\text{FV}] = \frac{C\left[(1+r)^t - 1 \right]}{r}$$

Note that this formula accounts for payments or contributions that occur at the end of each time period. If your contributions are more frequent than once a year, then for simplicity (the abovementioned formula is already complicated enough and this isn't a textbook) you can use your annualized value for C.

Rearranging the abovementioned equation can provide the required regular contribution (C) in order to hit your savings goals (use $n = 1$ for annual contributions):

$$C = \frac{[\text{FV}] \cdot r}{(1+r)^t - 1}$$

The monthly interest owed on a loan balance is:

$$I = \frac{P \cdot i}{12}$$

As expected, the loan payment (*PMT*) depends on the amount borrowed (*P*), interest rate (*i*), compounding frequency (*n*), and duration of the loan.

$$[\text{PMT}] = \frac{P \cdot \dfrac{i}{n}}{1 - \left(1 + \dfrac{i}{n}\right)^{-nt}}$$

Setting the payment and solving for P provide the total borrowed amount for a given payment and other loan conditions.

$$P = [\text{PMT}]\frac{1-\left(1+\dfrac{i}{n}\right)^{-nt}}{i\big/n}$$

The Net Present Value (NPV) formula for a constant stream of income or payments (C) is similar to the Future Value (FV) formula but with a negative exponent.

$$[\text{NPV}] = \sum_{k=1}^{t}\left[c(1+r)^{-k}\right] \Rightarrow [\text{NPV}] = \frac{c\left[1-(1+r)^{-t}\right]}{r}$$

The Ineffectiveness of the Catch-Up Contribution

Figure A.4 shows the account balances and contributions over a 35-year working period. The assumed growth rate is 7%.

Time	Standard Max		Max with Catch-Up		Forward Tiered with Catch-Up		Forward Tiered No Catch-Up		Tiered Reverse	
1	$ 23,500	$ 23,500	$ 23,500	$ 23,500	$ 5,500	$ 5,500	$ 5,500	$ 5,500	$ 23,500	$ 23,500
2	$ 23,500	$ 48,645	$ 23,500	$ 48,645	$ 6,250	$ 12,135	$ 6,250	$ 12,135	$ 22,750	$ 47,895
3	$ 23,500	$ 75,550	$ 23,500	$ 75,550	$ 7,000	$ 19,984	$ 7,000	$ 19,984	$ 22,000	$ 73,248
4	$ 23,500	$ 104,339	$ 23,500	$ 104,339	$ 7,750	$ 29,133	$ 7,750	$ 29,133	$ 21,250	$ 99,625
5	$ 23,500	$ 135,142	$ 23,500	$ 135,142	$ 8,500	$ 39,673	$ 8,500	$ 39,673	$ 20,500	$ 127,099
6	$ 23,500	$ 168,102	$ 23,500	$ 168,102	$ 9,250	$ 51,700	$ 9,250	$ 51,700	$ 19,750	$ 155,746
7	$ 23,500	$ 203,369	$ 23,500	$ 203,369	$ 10,000	$ 65,319	$ 10,000	$ 65,319	$ 19,000	$ 185,648
8	$ 23,500	$ 241,105	$ 23,500	$ 241,105	$ 10,750	$ 80,641	$ 10,750	$ 80,641	$ 18,250	$ 216,893
9	$ 23,500	$ 281,483	$ 23,500	$ 281,483	$ 11,500	$ 97,786	$ 11,500	$ 97,786	$ 17,500	$ 249,576
10	$ 23,500	$ 324,687	$ 23,500	$ 324,687	$ 12,250	$ 116,881	$ 12,250	$ 116,881	$ 16,750	$ 283,796
11	$ 23,500	$ 370,915	$ 23,500	$ 370,915	$ 13,000	$ 138,063	$ 13,000	$ 138,063	$ 16,000	$ 319,662
12	$ 23,500	$ 420,379	$ 23,500	$ 420,379	$ 13,750	$ 161,477	$ 13,750	$ 161,477	$ 15,250	$ 357,288
13	$ 23,500	$ 473,305	$ 23,500	$ 473,305	$ 14,500	$ 187,280	$ 14,500	$ 187,280	$ 14,500	$ 396,798
14	$ 23,500	$ 529,936	$ 23,500	$ 529,936	$ 15,250	$ 215,640	$ 15,250	$ 215,640	$ 13,750	$ 438,324
15	$ 23,500	$ 590,532	$ 23,500	$ 590,532	$ 16,000	$ 246,735	$ 16,000	$ 246,735	$ 13,000	$ 482,007
16	$ 23,500	$ 655,369	$ 23,500	$ 655,369	$ 16,750	$ 280,756	$ 16,750	$ 280,756	$ 12,250	$ 527,997
17	$ 23,500	$ 724,745	$ 23,500	$ 724,745	$ 17,500	$ 317,909	$ 17,500	$ 317,909	$ 11,500	$ 576,457
18	$ 23,500	$ 798,977	$ 23,500	$ 798,977	$ 18,250	$ 358,413	$ 18,250	$ 358,413	$ 10,750	$ 627,559
19	$ 23,500	$ 878,406	$ 23,500	$ 878,406	$ 19,000	$ 402,502	$ 19,000	$ 402,502	$ 10,000	$ 681,488
20	$ 23,500	$ 963,394	$ 23,500	$ 963,394	$ 19,750	$ 450,427	$ 19,750	$ 450,427	$ 9,250	$ 738,442
21	$ 23,500	$1,054,332	$ 23,500	$1,054,332	$ 20,500	$ 502,457	$ 20,500	$ 502,457	$ 8,500	$ 798,633
22	$ 23,500	$1,151,635	$ 23,500	$1,151,635	$ 21,250	$ 558,879	$ 21,250	$ 558,879	$ 7,750	$ 862,288
23	$ 23,500	$1,255,749	$ 23,500	$1,255,749	$ 22,000	$ 620,000	$ 22,000	$ 620,000	$ 7,000	$ 929,648
24	$ 23,500	$1,367,152	$ 23,500	$1,367,152	$ 22,750	$ 686,150	$ 22,750	$ 686,150	$ 6,250	$1,000,973
25	$ 23,500	$1,486,352	$ 23,500	$1,486,352	$ 23,500	$ 757,681	$ 23,500	$ 757,681	$ 5,500	$1,076,541
26	$ 23,500	$1,613,897	$ 31,000	$1,621,397	$ 31,000	$ 841,718	$ 23,500	$ 834,218		$1,151,899
27	$ 23,500	$1,750,370	$ 31,000	$1,765,895	$ 31,000	$ 931,639	$ 23,500	$ 916,114		$1,232,532
28	$ 23,500	$1,896,396	$ 31,000	$1,920,507	$ 31,000	$1,027,853	$ 23,500	$1,003,742		$1,318,809
29	$ 23,500	$2,052,643	$ 31,000	$2,085,943	$ 31,000	$1,130,803	$ 23,500	$1,097,504		$1,411,126
30	$ 23,500	$2,219,828	$ 31,000	$2,262,959	$ 31,000	$1,240,959	$ 23,500	$1,197,829		$1,509,905
31	$ 23,500	$2,398,716	$ 31,000	$2,452,366	$ 31,000	$1,358,827	$ 23,500	$1,305,177		$1,615,598
32	$ 23,500	$2,590,127	$ 31,000	$2,655,032	$ 31,000	$1,484,944	$ 23,500	$1,420,039		$1,728,690
33	$ 23,500	$2,794,935	$ 31,000	$2,871,884	$ 31,000	$1,619,891	$ 23,500	$1,542,942		$1,849,698
34	$ 23,500	$3,014,081	$ 31,000	$3,103,916	$ 31,000	$1,764,283	$ 23,500	$1,674,448		$1,979,177
35	$ 23,500	$3,248,567	$ 31,000	$3,352,190	$ 31,000	$1,918,783	$ 23,500	$1,815,159		$2,117,720

Figure A.4 The ineffectiveness of the catch-up contribution data

Notes

1. https://www.usinflationcalculator.com/inflation/historical-inflation-rates/.
2. https://www.calculator.net/investment-calculator.html.
3. https://ir.lendingclub.com/news/news-details/2023/Consumer-Emergency -Expenses-Rise-16-Year-Over-Year-to-1700-Far-Exceeding-The-400- Benchmark/default.aspx.
4. https://www.irs.gov/retirement-plans/roth-iras.
5. https://www.worlddata.info/america/usa/inflation-rates.php.
6. https://www.zippia.com/advice/american-savings-statistics/.
7. https://www.bls.gov/news.release/pdf/wkyeng.pdf.
8. https://www.ynab.com/.
9. Since 1963, there has not been any 8-year period where average home prices ended below what they started at. The average duration of homeownership for any given home in the United States is approximately 13 years (https:// www.nar.realtor/blogs/economists-outlook/how-long-do-homeowners -stay-in-their-homes).
10. https://friday.app/p/5-25-rule.
11. https://www.experian.com/blogs/ask-experian/identity-theft-statistics/.
12. https://www.fdic.gov/.
13. https://www.experian.com/.
14. https://www.equifax.com/.
15. https://www.transunion.com/.
16. https://www.investopedia.com/terms/p/primerate.asp.
17. https://www.investopedia.com/articles/retirement/08/borrow-from-401k -loan.asp.
18. https://www.ssa.gov/oact/cola/cbb.html.
19. https://www.irs.gov/taxtopics/tc751.
20. https://www.irs.gov/pub/irs-pdf/fw4.pdf.
21. https://www.irs.gov/taxtopics/tc551.
22. https://www.investopedia.com/terms/m/magi.asp.
23. https://www.nerdwallet.com/article/investing/fiduciary.
24. https://www.cfp.net/.
25. Cap refers to the "market capitalization" of the stock, which is the total shares multiplied by the current price.
26. https://www.investopedia.com/articles/investing/030916/buffetts- bet-hedge-funds-year-eight-brka-brkb.asp.
27. https://www.acorns.com/.

28. https://www.irs.gov/retirement-plans/retirement-plan-and-ira-required
    -minimum-distributions-faqs.
29. A rollover is done from an external account such as a 401(k) to your Roth
    IRA, while a conversion is done internally from your Traditional or Pretax
    IRA to your Roth IRA. They are essentially the same thing and have the
    same tax implications.
30. https://www.forbes.com/advisor/retirement/mega-backdoor-roth/.
31. https://fsastore.com/fsa-eligibility-list.
32. https://www.irs.gov/retirement-plans/plan-sponsor/simplified-employee
    -pension-plan-sep.
33. https://www.irs.gov/retirement-plans/one-participant-401k-plans.
34. https://www.investopedia.com/articles/investing/062714/100-minus
    -your-age-outdated.asp.
35. Report 1, rightmost column, first row: https://www.spglobal.com/spdji/en
    /documents/spiva/spiva-us-year-end-2020.pdf.
36. https://www.nerdwallet.com/article/investing/social-security/average
    -retirement-age-us.
37. https://www.cdc.gov/nchs/pressroom/nchs_press_releases/2022/2022
    0831.htm.
38. https://www.investopedia.com/terms/f/financial-independence-retire
    -early-fire.asp.
39. https://www.calculator.net/investment-calculator.html.
40. https://www.usa.gov/social-security.
41. https://www.ssa.gov/OACT/quickcalc/.
42. https://www.ssa.gov/benefits/calculators/.
43. https://www.dol.gov/general/topic/retirement.
44. https://www.investopedia.com/terms/f/fhaloan.asp.
45. https://www.hud.gov/sites/documents/15-01mlatch.pdf.
46. https://www.bankrate.com/loans/loan-calculator/.
47. The average is 5.4% from 1963 to 2025, but we will be conservative. Note
    that inflation is approximately 2.5%, so while the conservative nominal
    property appreciation is 3%, the real inflation-adjusted appreciation is 0.5%.
48. Only 5.8% of the 5-year windows since 1963 showed a decline in home
    prices, based on data from https://fred.stlouisfed.org/series/ASPUS.
49. See Figure A.3 in the appendix.

About the Author

WARNING: Buying this book will build Scott's financial future in addition to yours! Are you sure you want to proceed?

Scott Gong is a personal finance aficionado, first-generation college student, mechanical engineer, and founder of Scott Gong Tutoring—a highly reputable education company that emphasizes the "why" so students can learn to solve complex problems independently and apply their knowledge in real life. His mentorship in academics, career development, and personal finance has helped guide hundreds of students from college into adulthood. His work across multiple disciplines and countless "money talks" with other young professionals gives him the breadth and depth of perspective to write *Personal Finance for Young Professionals* with conviction. Scott's middle-class upbringing and college education are relatable, and his income comes from a normal engineering job—not from selling a course or book, not from a trust fund or inheritance, not from social media, and not from getting lucky in the stock market or crypto. He built his financial foundation from the simple and applicable techniques presented in this book, and he hopes that you will too!

Index